Understanding E-government

Governments these days often boast about the efficiency of their electronic systems. Information and communication technologies (ICTs) apparently allow public service to become cheaper, faster and more democratic. E-government has become another buzzword, the shining future of the public realm. Critics claim, however, that ICTs' potential for democratic renewal is hampered by ancient assumptions of how governments should function. But which viewpoint is nearer the truth?

In this original and insightful volume, Vincent Homburg demonstrates how the use, form and impact of ICTs are, in fact, entwined within the socio-political, economic and institutional aspects already established by government and public administration. Evangelical or fatalistic perspectives are discredited to show the different realities in which ICTs play a role in our daily lives. Using case studies and vignettes from throughout Europe and the USA, the book analyses what these new technologies actually do, and how they are screened through varying layers of bureaucracy and convention.

This is a timely addition to our understanding of what is meant by e-government. It gets behind the political rhetoric. *Understanding E-government: Information systems in public administration* will be key reading for all students of public administration, political science, organization theory and information systems.

Vincent Homburg is Associate Professor in Public Administration at Erasmus University Rotterdam, the Netherlands. He has written extensively on information technology, e-government and information policy.

Understanding E-government

Information systems in
public administration

Vincent Homburg

LONDON AND NEW YORK

First published 2008
by Routledge
2 Park Square, Milton Park,
Abingdon, Oxon, OX14 4RN

Simultaneously published in the USA and Canada
by Routledge
270 Madison Avenue, New York, NY 10016

Routledge is an imprint of the Taylor and Francis Group, an informa business

© 2008 Vincent Homburg

Typeset by Keyword Group Ltd. in Times New Roman and Helvetica
Printed and bound by TJ International Ltd., Padstow, Cornwall

British Library Cataloguing in Publication Data
A catalogue record for this book is available from the British Library

Library of Congress Cataloging in Publication Data
Homburg, Vincent.
Information systems in public administration: understanding
e-government/Vincent Homburg. P. cm.
Includes bibliographical references.
I. Internet in public administration. I. Title.
JF1525.A8H66 2008
352.3′802854678—dc22
2007042301

ISBN13: 978–0–415–43094–4 pbk
ISBN13: 978–0–415–43093–7 hbk

ISBN10: 0–415–43094–1 pbk
ISBN10: 0–415–43093–3 hbk

Contents

Preface

This work is about a very odd couple: public administration and information and communication technology (ICT). Representatives of both worlds have long neglected one another, other than using overly stereotypical images of each other's disciplines. In fact I could observe this myself when I joined the Information Systems group of the Faculty of Management and Organization Science at Groningen (The Netherlands) in order to prepare a PhD thesis. I had been trained in public administration and policy sciences, and at the beginning my colleagues were rather confused with what they considered to be my preoccupation with aberrant political processes and 'irrational' behaviour in general. Having completed the PhD thesis, I joined the Public Administration group at Erasmus University Rotterdam. There, my colleagues desperately tried to persuade me of the irrelevance of technology for the study of policy processes and public administration. At the same time they held me personally responsible for everything that went wrong with their personal computers, Internet connections and mobile phones, of course.

This book is neither about deviant technologies, nor about irrational behaviour in public administration. Rather, it is an attempt to argue how specific information and communication technologies in public administration are shaped and crafted in accordance with prevailing interests, power structures and values, whereas at the same time the practices and values of public administration itself are challenged by the potential of ICTs.

I can only hope that this book helps to persuade those in charge of developing public administration curricula to pay attention to ICTs in public administration programmes, and that students of information systems are introduced to the wonderful world of public administration. Let us hope that future public executives and public managers will be better equipped to deal with the challenges of 'e-government' and 'e-governance', beyond using it as a hollow phrase to denote desired yet rather unspecified public management reforms.

I end this preface by mentioning Christopher Pollitt, now at the Catholic University of Leuven, and Victor Bekkers of Erasmus University and by thanking them for their encouragement and support. Christopher Pollitt encouraged me to write this book and his advice has without any trace of doubt improved the book. Thanks to Victor Bekkers, who read the manuscript once it was near the final stage, and whose support was indispensable throughout the writing process.

Vincent Homburg
Rotterdam, Dordrecht, The Netherlands
September 2007

1 Introduction

Key points

After reading this chapter, you will be able to

- describe technological determinism as a perspective on the relation between technology and society
- explain how ICT applications result in dilemmas when applied in the real world of public administration
- describe a social shaping of technology perspective as a view on the relation between technology and society
- explain the differences in perspective of the academic disciplines of *public administration*, *information systems* and *organization theory* with respect to ICT applications in public administration.

A puzzling but faulty question ... how do 'ICTs' affect public administration?

Many articles, books and policy documents on information and communication technologies (ICTs) begin with mantra-like sketches of ubiquitous, revolutionary effects of microelectronics-based, digital 'smart machines' (Zuboff, 1988). Apparently, they offer unlimited benefits to individuals, functional units, organizations, governments or even the fabric of our society. For example, Burstein and Klein (1995: 254) enthusiastically claim that '[t]here is no disagreement on the essentially revolutionary nature of the forces unleashed by the new technology'. Similarly, Tapscott (1995) has heralded the information revolution in glowing terms:

> Today, we are witnessing the early turbulent days of a revolution as signifi-cant as any other in human history. A new medium of human communication is emerging, one that may prove to surpass all previous revolutions – the printing press, the telephone, the television, the computer – in its impact on our economic and social life.
>
> (Tapscott, 1995: xiii)

Academic commentators have also speculated about the advantages of ICT. They see the potential for increased levels of social interaction among 'empowered' individuals (Katz et al., 2001) or of new hourglass-shaped organizational structures enabling the elimination of middle management and drastically increasing levels of productivity (Leavitt and Whisler, 1958; Scott-Morton, 1991). Not to mention the emergence of virtual organizations (Groth, 1999) or interpretations of ICT representing even greater historical change for the fabric of society than the discrete, mechanical technologies of the industrial revolution (Castells, 2000). Even more than in previous eras, information and communication technologies, in the form of all kinds of smart machines, would appear to have *infused* our daily lives, organizations and societal structures (Bekkers and Homburg, 2005; Lips et al., 2004).

Above-mentioned claims are consistent with a line of reasoning known as 'technological determinism' (MacKenzie and Wajcman, 1985). Technological determinism depicts technology as a *cause* of social (or sometimes even historical) change. It views development of technology as a process that occurs independently and autonomously, separate from politics, economics and power. Technological progress is, in this view, inevitable, and is limited only by scarcity of material resources. Note that although many technological determinists stress progress, more efficient and effective operations, increased democratic value in the way governments function, and in general, more open, transparent societies, such 'utopian' visions are not necessarily a part of technological determinism. Beside these techno-optimists, there are also techno-pessimists who talk about the end of privacy and individual freedoms, increased potentials for surveillance and control by governments (and large corporations) and decreases in well-being (or inequalities in distribution of wealth among various groups in societies, the emergence of a digital divide that widens existing gaps in society).

For the public sphere, the above rhetorical sublime of technological progress (Mosco, 2004) has led to equivalent speculations about the nature and challenges of so-called electronic governments and electronic governance. For instance, the Organization for Economic Cooperation and Development (OECD) quite energetically promotes the use of ICTs in order to enable governments to reorganize their internal structures, focus more on citizens' demands and in general, increase their performance (OECD, 2003). Referring to ICTs' potential role in community development, former United Nations Secretary General Kofi Annan has stated that ICTs are powerful tools with diverse applications, and the challenge is to put that power at the service of all humankind.[1] In various countries, national policies have been drafted in which a 'wired' government takes shape (Minister for the Cabinet Office, 1999, 2000; National Audit Office, 2002; OECD, 2003). In Australian, Canadian and British policy documents, for example, information and communication technologies are portrayed as enablers of a less fragmented, more responsive, *joined-up* government. In Danish national e-government policy documents, the emphasis is on goals of free access to information, individual freedom for citizens to exercise influence, openness in the public sector and rationalization of service delivery. The picture that emerges from these policies is that smart technology is transforming, or is about to transform, the fabric of our society, including the machinery of public administration and governance. This picture is somewhat overstated and overly simplistic.

The claim that *smart machines transform public administration* is certainly an interesting one and – at first sight – it raises the question what the exact effects are and will be for public administration and government. As stated above, however, such a claim is unsatisfactory since it cannot be proven or disproven, and in general is not either plausible or questionable. There are at least two reasons why the claim is unsatisfactory.

First, it uses a very abstract notion of technology. It is not immediately clear what kind of technology is being reasoned about, what properties of technologies are important and how the technology is applied and implemented in specific contexts. Rhetorically, keeping technology abstract in the claim enables the focus to remain primarily upon desirable effects. In order to reason about the consequences of ICTs, it is necessary to open the ICT 'black box' implicit to many of the claims that try to envisage the future of smart machinery in public administration.

Second, the effects, impacts or consequences of ICTs are depicted in a rather exogenous way. Authors talk about increased efficiency (Gurbaxani and Wang, 1991), increased speed of operations and government transparency, without specifying how these eventual effects are accomplished, in what contexts the effects are likely to occur, and the kinds of effects that interfere with existing political, socio-organizational and institutional settings.

Case vignette 1.1: E-government pay-off in Europe

In a study on the pay-off of technology initiatives in government (TNO and CapGemini, 2004), it was concluded that ICTs do pay off in terms of improved quality of information provision, reduction of process time, reduction of administrative burdens, cost reduction, improved service level, increased efficiency and increased customer satisfaction. At least some of the changes not only occurred because of characteristics of the ICTs used in policy implementation (faster calculations, increased capacity to process huge amounts of information), but also could be attributed to organizational changes in back offices (for instance, redesign of workflows).

The focus of this book is upon the use of smart machines, or in general information and communication technologies, in and around public administration. In recent years, a lot has been said about 'electronic government' or 'e-government' (Bekkers and Homburg, 2005; Fountain, 2001; Grönlund, 2003; Snellen, 1998; Tat-Kei Ho, 2002) and in practice, there are enough existing implementations of ICTs to talk about an actual 'wired government' (Minister for the Cabinet Office, 1999, 2000; Ministerie van Economische Zaken, 1999; Ministry of Research and

Information Technology, 1995; Ministry of the Interior and Kingdom Relationships, 1999; National Audit Office, 2002; National Performance Review, 2000; OECD, 2003). It is seductive to ask the question what the effects of smart machines are for public administration, but, for the reasons mentioned above, such a question will not be asked in this book. Rather, the focus is on the properties, potentials and paradoxes of 'smart machines' for governments (including an analysis of what would make machines 'smart' or 'intelligent'). After reading the book, it will probably not be possible to give an answer to the question, what are the exact consequences of ICTs for public administration, but I hope that the question is more circumscribed, defined more exactly and, therefore, better answerable.

Examples of wired public administration: challenges, problems and dilemmas

Introduction

As has been argued above, this book pays attention to the use of ICTs in and around public administration in a specific and particular way. One could ask the question whether this is needed. Aren't there enough fine textbooks out there completely devoted to applications of ICTs? Yes there are. Nevertheless, it can be argued that existing textbooks do not pay enough attention to either properties or characteristics of ICTs, to the various uses of technology, or to the socio-political and institutional contexts in which smart machines are implemented and yield effects. In order to illustrate the need for this book some examples of implementations of ICTs in and around public administrations are presented below. They include questions and dilemmas that, until now, have remained unsolved.

Levying of taxes: transparency versus law enforcement

Internationally, national and federal tax agencies have championed the race for the most successful 'wired' government services. For example, in 2004 the US Internal Revenue Service (IRS) was cited as most reliable government website,[2] and throughout the world tax agencies are seen as frontrunners of efficient, responsive and customer-oriented government agencies. Many agencies have not only reorganized their internal structures and information systems, but also redesigned the ways in which they communicate with the outside world. Contacts with citizens now take place using advanced, customer-friendly websites, while government agencies are cooperating more and more for the purpose of cross-checking citizens' data and fighting fraud. For citizens, this implies that the processes of requesting rebates and submitting personal information has been simplified, and there is less need to submit information that has already been supplied to tax agencies. Furthermore, through websites, tax agencies are able to offer customized information about tax laws, regulations and so on. The Dutch Tax Agency, for example, claims that all the background dossiers and materials that a professional tax inspector needs are online and available to citizens.

In short, one could conclude that tax agencies have, over the past years, embraced ICTs and that these ICTs have yielded organizational transparency, customer orientation and efficiency.

There is, however, a limit to the technologically enabled customer orientation of tax agencies. In the past some tax agencies (for example, the Dutch Belastingdienst) have experimented with personalized web services, with which individual taxpayers could monitor the progress and status of tax filings. Comparable 'track and trace' services exist on almost every e-commerce application (for instance, e-banking services) and at first sight they appear desirable for tax agencies since they would be conducive to transparency and personalized customer orientation. This ignores the 'involuntary services' and enforcement role that tax agencies also provide. They are public service organizations as well as law enforcement agencies and the balancing of these functions provides a compelling argument against the use of 'track and trace' services. In their role of law enforcement agency, tax agencies try to maximize the citizen's *perceived* chance of being caught while trying to submit forged income figures or other kinds of information. A fully personalized service would reveal the actual checks and countermeasures available to tax agencies to fight fraud. Such a service could entice citizens to maximize calculative behaviour, which is of course not in the direct interest of tax agencies. This provides an example of the importance of how the specific context of ICT application shapes and interacts with the way that ICTs are implemented.

Focus on electronic service delivery may paradoxically widen gap between citizens and administration

Throughout the world, national and local governments are implementing web services to increase citizen orientation, reduce red tape, create one-stop shops, decrease the administrative burden on citizens and corporations, and increase citizens' trust in government (for a more complete discussion, refer to Chapter 6 on e-government). By increasing the quality of public service delivery, it is hoped to bridge the often-felt gap that exists between corporations and citizens on the one hand, and government agencies and administrations on the other hand.

Although it seems reasonable that citizens' trust increases as the level of quality of services increase, Fountain (2001) argues that the opposite might be the case. She notes that public organizations are not solely concerned with service delivery and points to the multifaceted (policy making and executive) character of many public sector organizations. Addressing citizens as consumers and defining government as a production company ignores the inherent political character of public service delivery. Public organizations delivering services are supposed to be not only responsive to the needs of customers, but also accountable to Good Citizens (Schudson, 1998) or *citoyens*, and to voters (Bekkers and Homburg, 2005). According to Fountain (2001), emphasizing service delivery and ignoring notions of citizenship, other than being a customer of public service, will eventually jeopardize legitimacy and citizens' trust in government.

Automating discretion: consequences for control and accountability

Many public sector services – for example specific benefits, permits or rebates – require some sort of interaction between public servants and citizens, at least until recently. Traditionally, human public service workers have been involved in applying regulations and routines to specific requests. Many of these workers can be qualified as *street-level bureaucrats:* public sector workers that interact directly with citizens and have considerable discretion in the way they organize the interaction, allocate facilities and possibly impose sanctions (Bovens and Zouridis, 2002; Lipsky, 1980). Being street-level bureaucrats, workers are both policy executors (they apply rules) as well as policy makers:

> the decisions of street-level bureaucrats, the routines they establish, and the devices they invent to cope with uncertainties and work pressures, effectively become the public policies they carry out. With others, I argue that it is a misconception to conceive of public policy as made in legislatures or top-floor suites of high-ranking administrators, because this neglects the impor-tant ways the policy gets made in the crowded offices and daily encounters of street level workers.
>
> (Lipsky, 1980: xii)

Notwithstanding that the discretionary powers of street-level bureaucrats are curtailed not only by generally prevailing laws, but also by material principles of sound administration – principle of careful preparation, and prohibition on *détournement de pouvoir* (abuse of power) – that can be used by the judiciary to correct behaviour by street-level bureaucrats.

Many executive organizations have implemented form processors, decision support systems and expert systems to automate the processes of issuing admin-istrative orders, thereby replacing or disciplining street-level bureaucrats, and squeezing their discretionary margins (Bovens and Zouridis, 2002). Some execu-tive processes have been fully automated. This transformation of execution can in part be seen as a process of rationalization, with which the predictability and control of executive processes have improved. Moreover, Bovens and Zouridis (2002) identify a new issue that has to do with the transfer of discretionary powers from street-level bureaucrats to system designers. With the emergence of fully automated executive processes, system designers have obtained the discre-tionary power to transform legal frameworks, regulations and organizational procedures into automated processes and programmes (Bovens and Zouridis, 2002). It is an empirical question how this shift of discretionary powers in executive organizations is to be translated into new forms of accountability and checks and balances. Bovens and Zouridis (2002) also ask the question whether a fully automated execution of laws can protect justice, since although digital rigidity may be a bureaucratic ideal, the absence of *Einzelfallgerechtigkeit* (individual cases) can lead to absurd, downright hazardous, and therefore undemocratic situations.

Institutional filter for technological innovation: expert systems in social administration

In the beginning of the 1990s, academics from Twente University in the Netherlands recognized that street-level bureaucrats working in social administration had severe difficulties with the administration of welfare programmes. They developed an expert system (Tessec) to assist street-level bureaucrats.[3] Studies showed that the quality of decisions could be increased with promising possibilities for the application of the system in the execution of the National Assistance Act, and in the administration of housing allowances. However, actual implementation was never achieved (apart from a few pilot projects), since the Tessec system never reached the status of an operational system in the standing organization of municipal social service organizations.[4] Much to the surprise (and possibly frustration) of the developers, during the 1990s a commercial developer (MRE) introduced an expert system that got a foothold in the market and grew within a few years to become the market leader. The MRE expert system functionally resembled the Tessec system. While the marketing strategies of MRE and technological proficiency of the system outperformed the Tessec approach, this is not sufficient to explain why MRE proved to be so successful and Tessec failed in practice. Svensson (2002) has demonstrated that the failure of the Tessec system, and acceptance of the comparable MRE system a few years later, had everything to do with the institutional context and rapid changes that occurred in this context. In the 1990s, fighting fraud and preventing abuse was put on the public agenda (see also Homburg, 1999). Following various reports, the formal requirements for the administration of welfare provision had been tightened. The municipalities were required from that moment on to comply with rules and validation procedures set by accountants and national inspectorates, and these actors, particularly accountants, strongly advocated the application of expert systems. Municipalities that opted for manual administration ran the risk of very thorough and intensive reviews of individual material files, with the likelihood that errors would be found and sanctioned. In conclusion, the actual use of expert systems in social administration can only to a limited degree be explained in terms of the purely technological properties of either Tessec or the MRE system. Decisive was the change in the socio-political climate with respect to how the National Assistance Act should be executed, and the rising dominance of accountants who favoured the use of expert systems. In other words, the institutional context served as a filter for technological innovation.

A social shaping of technology perspective

The above examples of applications of ICTs, in and around public administration, and of a 'wired' public administration, demonstrate that technologies do not directly and exogenously affect public administration. Rather, the anecdotal evidence illustrates how technology, and the transformation potential that is intrinsically embedded in information and communication technologies, interacts with, or is shaped by, values, norms, rules, beliefs and taken-for-granted assumptions of public administration.

Case vignette 1.2: Moses' bridge as iconic exemplar of technology–society interrelations

One of the most intensively discussed case studies in the literature on the relation between technology and society is provided by Langdon Winner. In his article 'Do artifacts have politics?', Winner (1980) discusses the question whether technological artefacts can have political values built into them. Although Winner focuses on the politics of built concepts like bridges and buildings, the discussion pertains to other technologies (such as nanotechnology, medical technology, but also information and communication technology) as well.

The main character in Winner's parable is Robert Moses (1888–1981), a senior official working for the New York City and New York State governments from roughly 1930 to 1960. Moses never held elected office, yet he is regarded as one of the most influential figures (a 'political entrepreneur', according to Joerges (1999)) in shaping the built environment of New York City and New York State. Using vast amounts of New Deal funds, Moses spearheaded the construction of (in no particular order) the United Nations Headquarters, Shea Stadium, the Triborough Bridge, the Van Wyck Expressway, the Whitestone Expressway, the Henry Hudson Parkway, the Long Island Expressway, the Robert Moses Power Dam at Niagara, the Robert Moses Power Dam at Massena, the Grand Central Parkway, the Southern State Parkway, the Northern State Parkway, Downing Stadium, the Major Deegan Expressway, the Alexander Hamilton Bridge, the Throgs Neck Bridge, the Cross Bay Bridge and the Bronx-Whitestone Bridge (Caro, 1975). Apart from being involved in infrastructural and housing projects, Moses, an avid swimmer, also initiated and directed the construction of many pools and State Parks with access to beaches.

In his analysis, Winner focuses on accessibility of Jones Beach, a State Park that is considered to be one of the most prestigious State Parks Moses ever helped to develop. Winner described how Moses attempted to improve the accessibility of Jones Beach by designing bridges that connected New York City to Long Beach. The bridges were built very low, so that automobiles could pass but public buses could not. Furthermore, Moses used his power to veto the extension of the Long Island Rail Road to Long Beach, thus further complicating access to the beach for poor citizens. Winner argues that the bridges prevented the lower strata of the population (especially African Americans) going to the beaches.

Winner's interpretation was that Moses had intentionally designed the bridges in such a way that African Americans were discouraged to go to the beach. Moreover, he uses this case study to demonstrate how technology puts constraints on specific behaviour (note the analogy with the American political scientist Robert Dahl's definition of power: 'A has power over B to the extent that he can get B to do something that B would not otherwise do') and thus how technology and technical artefacts are intrinsically political.

It must be noted here that Winner's interpretation and conclusions are contested (Joerges, 1999; Woolgar and Cooper, 1999). For example Joerges asks the question whether Moses was indeed an explicit racist, like Winner (who followed Caro's biography of Moses) makes us believe, or whether Winner had merely created 'a particularly well constructed artifact, capable of serving a great number of rhetorical purposes' (Joerges, 1999: 424). Joerges argues that

1   Winner and Caro were wrong in the sense that the bridges were not primarily meant to discourage buses to pass through; in fact, buses were not allowed to enter State Parks anyway and there were alternative roads between New York City and Long Beach.
2   Moses presumably wanted to preserve the Long Island landscape he knew from his childhood and to prevent commercialization and ecological destruction as much as possible through alliances with Long Island aristocracy and through benevolent state control.
3   The relation between control (access) rights and building form is not as straightforward as apparent at first sight; Joerges tones down the role of designers, and highlights how various other actors (other than merely the designers) decide over and over again which meanings and uses are inscribed in technology.

In Joerges' line of reasoning, technology is not so much a cause of social effects, but rather a medium of mediation, negotiation and translation of expectations, demands, preferences and requirements of *many* people or organizations that are – over time – involved with technology, in this case bridges.

In the previous section, it was shown that:

- goal diversity (service delivery and law enforcement) limits the application of personalized portals in the case of tax agencies;
- electronic service delivery may very well bias a limited conception of the role of citizens, thereby paradoxically endangering citizen's trust;

- automating the process of applying rules and regulations may eventually affect procedures for bureaucratic control and accountability;
- institutions filter technological innovations (like the case of expert systems in Dutch local social administration).

In the chapters to come, technological determinism's assumption that technology on the one hand and economy, power and politics on the other hand are independent is relaxed. Information and communication technologies are assumed to be simultaneously social and physical artefacts (Orlikowkski and Barley, 2001). They are physical in the sense that they are designed to meet engineering requirements and reflect assumptions on how technology should be applied in the real world of public administration. They are also social, in the sense that every technology that is put to use constrains and allows specific uses by specific actors (Fulk et al., 1987; Homburg, 1999; Markus, 1983), and shapes and is shaped by the institutions that surround public administration (Bekkers and Homburg, 2005; Snellen, 1998; Zouridis, 2000). Consequently, what is traditionally considered as 'the technology' and its 'institutional context' are often hard to demarcate. What is pursued in this book is an understanding of how information and communication technologies are embedded in complex socio-political networks of governments and governance, and how they are shaped by institutional characteristics. This conforms to an existing field, known within the literature as the 'social shaping of technology' (MacKenzie and Wajcman, 1985; Williams and Edge, 1996).[5]

One of the many implications of using a social shaping of technology perspective, is that the effects or consequences of the application of information and communication technologies are not necessarily to be noted in terms of improvements (or perhaps decline) of rationality, but rather may result in dilemmas because norms and values of public administration may conflict and contradict one another. The perspective adopted here does assume a role for technology and technological development, but especially focuses on how technology (either in design, or in actual use) interacts with norms and values of the context in which it is applied.

Theoretical lenses used in this book

In this book, 'smart machines' are simultaneously social and physical artefacts, therefore it is assumed that eventual effects do not result solely from properties of the technology. Rather, it is assumed that effects are intrinsically linked with public administration's socio-political and institutional context (Fulk et al., 1987; Homburg, 1999; Markus, 1983). In order to cope with this variety, various theoretical perspectives are used (Gazendam, 1993; Orlikowkski and Barley, 2001). They are introduced below, and, with the risk of being overly stereotypical, confronted and contrasted.

The discipline of information systems

Information systems as a discipline used to go by various names in the past: computer machinery, electronic data processing, management information systems, information management and e-business, to name a few. The discipline has long centred on the development, implementation and impact of information and communication technology in and between organizations (Homburg, 1999).

In a way, the discipline of information systems mainly focuses on the physical aspect of ICTs, and emphasizes *engineering*. As in other branches of engineering (like mechanical engineering, civil engineering or chemical engineering), the objective of information system engineers is to design methodologies, solutions to problems and to find out 'what works', given *functional* requirements and constraints in time and money. The problems and solutions information systems engineers are confronted with, should be contextually, materially and temporally bounded (Orlikowkski and Barley, 2001). However, apart from being concerned with engineering, information systems scholars have also contributed to studying consequences of ICT for deskilling or re-skilling labour in organizations (Attewell and Rule, 1984), for centralization or decentralization in organizations (George and King, 1991) and for organizations' performance in general (Gurbaxani and Wang, 1991).

The most important contribution of the discipline of information systems to the core theme of this book is the recognition of the variety in technologies that exists, and the variety of ways in which technologies can be designed and implemented. It matters whether technology is designed as a rational *total system* that is supposed to control and monitor specific processes. Or alternatively, whether it is implemented as *end-using computing*, thereby appealing to and taking into account the requirements, needs and annoyances of individuals carrying out specific tasks.

Over the years, information systems as a discipline has incorporated and shown sensitivity towards concepts like the cognitive, political and strategic dynamics of social settings (Orlikowkski and Barley, 2001). There is, however, still a blind spot for questions about how institutions shape the design and use of ICTs (probably with the exception of King et al., 1994). If one looks at the specific effects ICTs have upon, let's say organizational structures, institutional arrangements or on society at large, one finds that these effects are dealt with briefly in final, reflective chapters of information system textbooks, or in very short concluding sections in chapters.

The discipline of organization theory

The focus of organization theory traditionally is different from the focus of the discipline of information systems. In particular, an important difference is that the epistemology of organization theory more closely resembles traditional science (as opposed to engineering). The objective is to develop explanatory theories about human behaviour in and between organizations, and confront theoretical expectations with empirical data. Some theorists add normative connotations to explanatory organization theories.

Organization theorists have, over the past century or so, developed theories of organizational structure, culture, organizational decision making and learning, strategy formation, power struggles, to name just a few subjects. Their objectives have been to explain differences in terms of organizational performance, viability, innovativeness, and so forth. Organization theory's most important contribution to the theme of this book is that it enables the analysis of intra-organizational processes and human behaviour in organizational arrangements.

Over the years, technology (including information technology) has played an important role in the various organization theories. ICTs figure prominently in theories on organizational learning and in contingency theory, although this has been in a rather abstract way. For example, in the once rather influential contingency stream in organization theory, the focus with respect to technology was limited to the decision of whether or not to adopt specific technologies. Once adopted, they were assumed to produce effects in organizations (Orlikowkski and Barley, 2001). According to Orlikowski and Barley, this also applies to contingency theorists, as well as subsequent scholars working with socio-technical design, social choice theory and so forth.

The discipline of public administration

Public administration as a discipline is concerned with the analysis of societal (collective) problems, processes of collective decision making and processes by which decisions are implemented. Traditionally, the discipline has focused on the role of governments in the above-mentioned processes. Increasingly, however, the discipline of public administration in Western countries focuses on the interplay between various government institutions and non-governmental organizations, interest groups, financial institutions, corporations, individual citizens, etc.

The discipline of public administration addresses themes like regulation, the participation of societal actors in policy making and policy implementation, issues of public and political accountability for collective action, and so on (Bellamy and Taylor, 1998; Lips et al., 2004). In general, the discipline of public administration is more focused on societal steering and governance, whereas organization theory is focused on internal processes of organizations (including public sector organizations).

The discipline of public administration suffers in part from the same problems with respect to technology as the discipline of organization theory. The role of information and communication technologies is not fully incorporated in its theories or lines of reasoning, exceptions notwithstanding (Bekkers, 1998; Bekkers and Homburg, 2005; Danziger and Viborg Andersen, 2002; Snellen, 1998). For example, Gruening (2001) thoroughly analysed the origins in 14 schools of thought in the discipline of public administration, and concluded 'the *use of information technology* seems to be a characteristic ... that has no specific theoretical roots. It is strictly a pragmatic idea, used where it is useful' (Gruening, 2001: 17). The renowned public administration scientists, Christopher Pollitt and Geert Bouckaert, remark that technological progress will *sometimes* be helpful to public administration. However, they also argue that quality of implementation is an empirical question and that technological progress may prove to be a more important ingredient for the *rhetoric* of management reform in public administration (Pollitt and

Bouckaert, 2000). Dunleavy and Margetts (2000) remark that this is all Pollitt and Bouckaert have to say on ICTs in a book over 300 pages long.

A programme for this book

In the remainder of this book, several themes regarding the use of information and communication technologies ('smart machines') in and around public administration will be dealt with. The theoretical lenses described in the previous section will be instrumental to this analysis.

I began this book with the concept of 'smart machines' and the idea of intelligent machinery that is often associated with modern ICTs. In this introductory chapter, a specific view ('social shaping') of technology was presented, in which the emphasis is on how norms and values of public administration interact with technology, including technology's proclaimed potential for transformation. Characteristics of contemporary information and communication technologies, and avenues for actual smart machines, are explored in Chapter 2. In this chapter, confrontations and interactions between properties of technology and institutions are identified and reflected upon.

Chapter 3 takes a different angle and reflects on technology from a point of view of the Information Society. Thus having reflected upon the interrelation between technology and society at rather macro levels of analysis, Chapter 4 analyses how one of the cornerstones of the discipline of public administration, the bureaucracy, contests and is contested by ICTs. Chapter 5 elaborates these discussions by focusing on how relations between various organizations shape and are shaped by technology. E-government as a contemporary phenomenon, and ways in which e-government is shaped in various jurisdictions, is described in Chapter 6. Chapter 7 focuses on a specific issue, the evaluation of ICT in public administration. Conclusions and reflections are presented in Chapter 8.

Discussion questions

1   The academic discipline of public administration has long neglected information and communication technologies. Why do you think this is so, and why has this changed since the mid-1990s or so?
2   In White Papers and other policy documents, there are often claims in which technological determinist elements can be discerned ('ICTs will ... transform governments'). Why do you think these lines of argumentation are so attractive to politicians and administrators?
3   What are important differences (in terms of epistemology) between the academic disciplines of public administration, organization theory and information systems? What are implications for the study of ICTs in each of these disciplines?
4   Think of an example of how specific instantiations of information technology (a municipal website, law enforcement database management system,

electronic public discussion forum) can have political significance. Discuss whether the political meaning has been designed by developers, or has developed in the actual use of the system.

Notes

1 http://www.apdip.net/ (last visited 9 February 2006).
2 http://www.irs.gov/newsroom/article/0,,id=130492,00.html (last visited 9 February 2006).
3 Tessec is the Twente Expert System for Social Security, an expert system to be used in the administration of municipal social service departments.
4 One of the developers, Jörgen Svensson, stated that the failure of the Tessec system in terms of operational application can be explained by the dominant command perspective on law, thereby ignoring administrative practice in municipal agencies. The eventual success of the MRE expert system in comparable contexts is therefore even more surprising.
5 In this volume, I use a rather liberal conception of social shaping of technology. It does not follow particular consensual orthodoxies, claiming distinctiveness of subdisciplines like social construction of technology, political economy of technology, or sociology of knowledge (Williams and Edge, 1996).

References

Attewell, P., and Rule, J. (1984). Computing and organizations: What we know and what we don't know. *Communications of the ACM, 27*(12), 1184–1191.
Bekkers, V. J. J. M. (1998). *Grenzeloze overheid. Over informatisering en grensveranderingen in het openbaar bestuur.* Alphen aan den Rijn: Samsom.
Bekkers, V. J. J. M., and Homburg, V. M. F. (eds) (2005). *The Information Ecology of E-Government.* Amsterdam: IOS Press.
Bellamy, C., and Taylor, J. (1998). *Governing in the Information Age.* Buckingham: Open University Press.
Bovens, M., and Zouridis, S. (2002). From street-level bureaucracy to system-level bureaucracy: How information and communication technology is transforming administrative discretion and constitutional control. *Public Administration Review, 62*(2), 174–184.
Burstein, D., and Klein, D. (1995). *Road Warriors: Dreams and Nightmares along the Information Superhighway.* New York: Dutton.
Caro, R. A. (1975). *The Power Broker: Robert Moses and the Fall of New York.* New York: Vintage.
Castells, M. (2000). Materials for an exploratory theory of the network society. *British Journal of Sociology, 51*(1), 5–24.
Danziger, J. N., and Viborg Andersen, K. (2002). Impacts of information technology on public administration: An analysis of empirical research from the golden age of transformation. *International Journal of Public Administration, 25*(5), 591–627.
Dunleavy, P., and Margetts, H. (2000). The advent of digital government: Public bureaucracies and the State in the Information Age. Paper presented at the Annual Conference of the American Political Science Association, Washington, DC.
Fountain, J. (2001). *Building the Virtual State.* Washington, DC: Brookings Institution.
Fulk, J., Steinfield, C. W., and Schmitz, J. (1987). A social information processing model of media use in organizations. *Communication Research, 14,* 529–552.

Gazendam, H. W. M. (1993). *Variety Controls Variety: The Use of Organization Theories in Information Management*. Groningen: Wolters-Noordhoff.

George, J. F., and King, J. L. (1991). Examining the computing and centralisation debate. *Communications of the ACM, 27*(7), 650–665.

Grönlund, A. (2003). Emerging electronic infrastructures (exploring democratic components). *Social Science Computer Review, 21*(1), 55–72.

Groth, L. (1999). Future organizational design. In L. Groth (ed.) *Future Organizational Design*. Chichester: Wiley.

Gruening, G. (2001). Origin and theoretical basis of New Public Management. *International Public Management Journal, 4*(1), 1–25.

Gurbaxani, V., and Wang, S. (1991). The impact of information systems on organizations and markets. *Communications of the ACM, 34*(1), 59–73.

Homburg, V. M. F. (1999). *The Political Economy of Information Management: A Theoretical and Empirical Analysis of Decision Making Regarding Interorganizational Information Systems*. Capelle aan den IJssel: Labyrinth.

Joerges, B. (1999). Do politics have artefacts? *Social Studies of Science, 29*(3), 411–431.

Katz, J., Rice, R., and Aspden, P. (2001). The Internet 1995–2000: Access, civic involvement and social interaction. *American Behavioural Scientist, 45*(3), 405–419.

King, J. L., Gurbaxani, V., Kraemer, K. L., McFarlan, W., Raman, K. S., and Yap, C. (1994). Institutional factors in information technology innovation. *Information System Research, 5*(2), 139–169.

Leavitt, H. J., and Whisler, T. L. (1958). Management in the 1980s. *Harvard Business Review, 36*(6), 41–48.

Lips, M., Bekkers, V. J. J. M., and Zuurmond, A. (eds) (2004). *ICT en Openbaar Bestuur*. Utrecht: Lemma.

Lipsky, M. (1980). *Street-Level Bureaucracy: Dilemmas of the Individual in Public Services*. New York: Russell Sage Foundation.

MacKenzie, D., and Wajcman, J. (eds) (1985). *The Social Shaping of Technology: How the Refrigerator Got ITs Hum*. Milton Keynes: Open University Press.

Markus, M. L. (1983). Power, politics and MIS implementation. *Communications of the ACM, 26*, 430–444.

Minister for the Cabinet Office (1999). *Modernising Government*. London: Minister for the Cabinet Office.

Minister for the Cabinet Office (2000). *E-Government: A Strategic Framework for Public Services in the Information Age*. London: Minister for the Cabinet Office.

Ministerie van Economische Zaken (1999). *De Digitale Delta*. The Hague: Ministerie van Economische Zaken.

Ministry of Research and Information Technology (1995). *From Vision to Action: Info-Society 2000*. Copenhagen: Ministry of Research and Information Technology.

Ministry of the Interior and Kingdom Relationships (1999). *Contract with the Future*. The Hague: Ministry of the Interior and Kingdom Relationships.

Mosco, V. (2004). *The Digital Sublime: Myth, Power and Cyberspace*. Cambridge, MA: MIT Press.

National Audit Office (2002). *Better Public Services through E-Government*. London: National Audit Office.

National Performance Review (2000). *Conversations with America: National Performance Review*.

OECD (2003). *The E-Government Imperative*. Paris: OECD.

Orlikowkski, W. J., and Barley, S. R. (2001). Technology and institutions: What can research on information technology and research on organizations learn from each other? *MIS Quarterly, 25*(2), 145–165.

Pollitt, C. P., and Bouckaert, G. (2000). *Public Management Reform: A Comparative Analysis*. Oxford: Oxford University Press.

Schudson, M. (1998). *The Good Citizen: A History of American Civic Life*. New York: The Free Press.

Scott-Morton, M. S. (1991). *The Corporation of the 1990s*. New York: Oxford University Press.

Snellen, I. T. M., and van de Donk, W. B. H. J (eds) (1998). *Public Administration in an Information Age*. Amsterdam: IOS Press.

Svensson, J. S. (2002). Legal expert systems in social administration: From fearing computers to fearing accountants. *Information Polity, 7*, 143–154.

Tapscott, D. (1995). *The Digital Economy: Promise and Peril in the Age of Networked Intelligence*. New York: McGraw-Hill.

Tat-Kei Ho, A. (2002). Reinventing local governments and the e-government initiative. *Public Administration Review, 62*(4), 434–444.

TNO and CapGemini (2004). *Does E-Government Pay Off?* Delft: TNO and CapGemini.

Williams, R., and Edge, D. (1996). The social shaping of technology. *Research Policy, 25*, 865–899.

Winner, L. (1980). Do artifacts have politics? *Daedalus, 109*(1), 121–136.

Woolgar, S., and Cooper, G. (1999). Do artefacts have ambivalence? Moses' bridges, Winner's bridges and other urban legends in ST and S. *Social Studies of Science, 29*(3), 433–449.

Zouridis, S. (2000). *Digitale disciplinering: over ICT, organisatie, wetgeving en het automatiseren van beschikkingen*. Tilburg: Katholieke Universiteit Brabant.

Zuboff, S. (1988). *In the Age of the Smart Machine: The Future of Work and Power*. New York: Basic Books.

2 On technology, intelligence and the social

Key points

After reading this chapter, you will be able to:

- describe the Turing machine as an abstract model of computer machinery, and describe actual information and communication technologies in terms of basic and functional characteristics
- explain the notion of computer intelligence using the Turing test and sum up objections against the Turing test
- explain how 'computer intelligence' relates to organizational and democratic intelligence.

Introduction

In Chapter 1, the focus was on the relation between information and communication technologies and public administration. One of the obstacles to any meaningful discussion of this intricate relation is the often rather abstract notion of information and communication technologies. Therefore, in this chapter, I will discuss relevant properties of ICTs, and focus on avenues for 'smart machines'. As will be made clear in this chapter, the label 'smart machines' is more than a fashionable term: the possibility of machine intelligence has also given rise to much academic, philosophical debate and even to the emergence of specific branches in the disciplines of law, computer science, cognitive sciences and philosophy, such as *artificial intelligence*. Moreover, machine intelligence and smart machines raise interesting questions for public administrations. For example, if smart machines actually existed, they would perhaps be able to enhance policy making and policy implementation. For the sake of discussion, you might think of a highly interactive municipal website (the non-existing site http://www.utopia.gov) to which citizens can turn to if they have questions regarding local government's services. Suppose it is possible for citizens to interact with the website using natural language, and that the website responds in a very adequate way: it answers questions satisfactorily, it explains why specific measures have been taken and what is required to apply for specific benefits or other services. Furthermore, it reminds citizens of services or obligations that may apply to specific situations. Would such an application be useful for citizens? I think most of us would agree. Does this make the website intelligent? I think most of us would disagree. But what if the website really comes up with valuable responses, unexpected solutions to citizens' problems *in a manner that is indistinguishable from the way in which a human, intelligent civil servant helps citizens*? Would this make the website and its underlying technology intelligent?

These questions may seem awkward at first sight, or only valid for the domain of science fiction novels and movies.[1] And indeed, the theme of machine intelligence is a theme that almost inevitably arouses forceful and emotional reactions. On the one hand, debates are sometimes dominated by discussants claiming that human intelligence is so unique it can never be emulated by artefacts (for a discussion, refer to Saygin et al., 2000). On the other hand, we see that computers nowadays execute complex legislation, and that perhaps, in the near future, computers may be able to judge court cases. Some authors, notably science fiction authors, but also scholars, even emphasize the need for an immutable moral code for intelligent machines, to prevent machine domination over human beings (Weizenbaum, 1979). Such a code is of course merely a thought experiment, but nevertheless it has been discussed thoroughly in the academic literature (Clarke, 1993, 1994; Hirose, 1996).

This chapter is structured as follows. First, the focus will be on what in essence computer machinery is, and what machine intelligence is. Second, functional characteristics of computer machinery are listed and explored. Then it is explained how machine intelligence relates to organizational intelligence. The extent to which ICTs can enhance societal, democratic intelligence is then dealt with. Conclusions are presented at the end.

The essence of computer machinery

The Turing machine

Before we can reflect on notions of smart machines and intelligent machinery, it may be wise to reflect on what a computer essentially is. The digital computers we are nowadays familiar with are in fact physical manifestations of an *abstract* machine called the Turing machine, which was proposed by the British mathematician Alan Mathison Turing (1912–1954). Alan Turing proposed the idea of the Turing machine in 1936, when he was a young Fellow of King's College, Cambridge University. It was a way to express in the simplest terms the essence of *computation* and to explore the concept of *algorithms*. It should be noted that initially, the Turing machine was nothing more than a thought experiment. At first, Turing thought of the 'machine' as a human being with pencil and paper attempting to carry out automated computation. While sounding simple, it was of vital importance to the idea of computing because a Turing machine could do anything that any other digital machine (including the most sophisticated supercomputers) could do.[2]

The abstract model of the Turing machine is digital and consists of input and output devices, a processor and memory.[3] In our contemporary practice, we would think of input devices as keyboards and mice, central processing units (CPUs) as chips with millions of transistors on it, memory as devices capable of storing billions of symbols, and output devices as monitors or printers. However, obviously, Turing was not aware of these types of technology, and in fact he was concerned only with the essence of computation. The Turing machine, as proposed by Turing, consists of two parts: an infinite paper tape with symbols written on it, and a head.[4] The head, in Turing's conceptualization, has a number of features.

- The head is able to write symbols on the tape.
- The head is able to read symbols on the tape.
- The head can remember what it has read.
- The head can erase (and rewrite) symbols on the tape.
- The head can move itself over the tape.

The Turing machine can perform calculation by performing the above steps in specific sequences. Basically, the machine manipulates the symbols on the tape, moving the head over the tape and changing its internal state, according to an algorithm (or program) that controls the behaviour of the head (partly depending on what symbol the head reads). The results of the manipulation are visible on the tape. The tape consists of symbols, which, together, can represent almost anything: numbers (so that a program can perform calculations), coded chess problems (so that the program can perform a move in a game), coded legal principles (so that the program can execute specific laws) and so on.

The Turing machine is obviously extremely simple, but it represents a basic model of computation and with that, a model of a general purpose machine that is designed to be used in a variety of situations and for a variety of purposes. Moreover, it is programmable, that is, it has the ability to be instructed (programmed) and to behave appropriately in specific situations that are represented on the tape (Simon, 2001). The most advanced computers that we tend to work with nowadays are machines that conform to the above description.

Before continuing our discussion on the question whether a Turing machine possesses the necessary and sufficient means to display intelligent behaviour, it should be emphasized that Turing not only contributed to the understanding of the essence of machine calculation, but also contributed to the design and construction of the first actual computer devices. From 1939 onwards, Turing had been confronted with the possibilities of electromagnetic relays. He realized the potential of this technology to implement logical operations in the context of the abstract Turing machine. While working at the British Government Code and Cipher School at Bletchley Park (near London), he identified an interesting field of application for machine computation: decrypting and code-breaking of encrypted German messages. Turing found out that electronic storage and electromagnetic relays proved to be effective and practical alternatives for his (imaginary, infinite) paper tape. Turing co-designed and engineered the first electronic digital computer, the 30-tons weighing Colossus.[5] The engineering principles underlying the Colossus computer paved the way for subsequent computer designs, which had been initially created especially for the military domain. Later on, they were also applied to civilian domains, such as processing statistics (census), registering information and making calculations in financial institutions.

For the discussion on smart machines and intelligent machinery, it should be noted that in the second half of the 1930s, Turing seemed to believe that human beings possessed *intuition* that enabled them to perform incomputable steps beyond the scope of the Turing machine. Turing's biographer, Andrew Hodges, commented that by 1941, however, Turing decided that computable operations were sufficient to account for 'non-mechanical' mental operations, and even for truth-recognition (Hodges, 2000).[6] These ideas eventually resulted in the 1950 article 'Computing machinery and intelligence' (Turing, 1950) in which Turing described and defined 'intelligent' machinery.[7]

Defining characteristics of computers

Referring to the basic concept of the Turing machine, and following John von Neumann (1903–1957), a Hungarian-born mathematician, who worked on ENIAC (see note 5), one can identify three essential characteristics of any (digital) computer: memory, binary digitization, and central processing (Barney, 2000).

Memory

In order to be able to function, computers must have a memory in which both data and sets of instructions (or programs) are stored. Storage media in actual computers are typically chips, magnetic disks, or optical devices such as CD or DVD rewriters. In order to qualify as a computer, a device must be able to allow for changes in data or programming without requiring the reconfiguration of hardware (Augarten, 1984).

Binary digitization

Binary digitization is the second defining characteristic. The physics of electronics operates to manipulate symbols more effectively if data is rendered into a series of binary digits (zeros and ones, which might represent, for example, 'false' and 'true'), or bits. Thankfully, numbers and binary values are not the only abstractions that can be converted into bits. Any finite set of values, representing students' grades, topographic maps, movies, architectural designs, econometric models, Acts, to name just a few examples, can be represented in this way. This *makes a computer much more than just a calculator* since it allows computers to store, display and manipulate various sources of information, not just mathematical wizardry. As Barney (2000) has described:

> Because of binary digitization, a computer can 'read' a list of items and add up a grocery bill; 'listen' to a Beethoven piano Sonata and instantly replay it

backward; 'look at' the *Mona Lisa* and immediately reproduce her with a frown; and 'sense' our entry in a darkened room and illuminate it more quickly than we can flip a switch.

(Barney, 2000: 64)

Central processing

The third defining characteristic is central processing. Central processing is basically the process of symbol manipulation that is required by adding things up in a grocery bill, playing backward a sonata or altering a painting. It consists of performing operations on streams of binary pairs that pass as inputs and outputs.[8] In practice, these processes take place within the CPU of a computer, for instance the Pentium processor of the computers that we are working with on a daily basis.

Much of the rapid developments in the computer industry have been driven by the pursuit of vaster amounts of memory in computers, and in processing speed in CPUs. The UNIVAC computer, the first computer to enter the commercial market in the 1950s, was sold for $200,000, had a memory capacity of 84,000 bits and could perform up to 8000 instructions per second. Any ordinary Pentium-based personal computer that is sold for a couple of hundreds of dollars or euros in the shops today has a memory capacity of billions of bits and processing speeds of approximately 300 million instructions per second. And yet the computers keep getting smaller.

Case vignette 2.1: Moore's Law

In 1965, microprocessor manufacturer Intel co-founder Gordon Moore observed that the density of transistors (microelectronics-based switches) on computer chips doubles every twelve months. This observation was given the name Moore's Law, and the prediction underlying the law has turned into a legend in writings on information and communication technology. Moore's Law was in fact supported by developments in the semiconductor industry. It was not until September 2007 that Gordon Moore himself at a corporate event of Intel declared that his Law would probably not be able to predict future developments of transistor density, as designers are confronted with limitations with respect to the atomic nature of matter.[9]

The implications of Moore's Law are not confined to questions of what chip layouts are feasible (or, more precisely, to matters of decreasing *costs* of transistors per square inch, which was what Moore was actually interested in). Moore himself was more interested in how decreasing costs of computing would result in ubiquitous computing power that seems to appear everywhere: not only in the machines we tend to name 'computer', but also in digital wristwatches, RFID (radio-frequency identification) chips that, for example, are attached to car components and that enable tracking and tracing of these components wherever they go, and in mobile phones (smartphones) whose computing power equals the computing power of personal computers of five years old, to name just a few examples.

The Turing test: does computation add up to intelligence?

The academic discipline of artificial intelligence centres on the question how to reason about and build machines that emulate human beings. The question has been asked long before the advent of the academic discipline, and even before Turing proposed the Turing machine. In as early as the seventeenth century, Descartes speculated on the possibility of smart machines:

> It is indeed conceivable that a machine could be so made that it would utter words, and even words appropriate to the presence of physical acts or objects which cause some change in its organs; as, for example, it was touched in some spot so that it would ask what you wanted to say to it; in another, that it would cry that it was hurt, and so on for similar things. But it could never modify its phrases to reply to the sense of whatever was said in its presence, as even the most stupid men can do.
>
> (Descartes, 1637/1985: 140)

Descartes emphasized the importance of ordinary conversation as a test for intelligence. So, intelligence can be thought of as requiring a number of abilities, among them the abilities to

- take coherent discourse (as opposed to isolated sentences) as input
- make inferences and revise beliefs
- understand plans and make plans for conversations (to ask and answer questions, to respond to questions and to initiate conversation)
- learn about the world and about language, in part via conversation
- have background ('world') knowledge and add to this base through conversation
- remember what it heard, learned, inferred and revised.

Case vignette 2.2: Can ICTs play chess and judge court cases?

Dutch professor (in law and in artificial intelligence) Jaap van den Herik projected in the beginning of the 1990s that by 2000, a computer would defeat the chess world champion, and that by 2005, the strongest computers will always win against human beings, whatever their strength. Although he was only partly right with respect to the game of chess (the chess program Deep Blue indeed defeated world champion Gary Kasparov in 1997, but since then computers have not always won against human chess players), this did not stop him in claiming that by 2080, ICTs will be able to judge court cases and that human judges could be replaced by machinery.

Van den Herik's line of argumentation rests on the principle that judging court cases involves legal reasoning based on rules laid out in Acts and jurisprudence, and by applying general rules to specific cases. If it is possible to model legal rules in artificial language, and to model cases and world knowledge, it will be possible, according to van den Herik, to automate legal reasoning (van den Herik, 1991).

Given the technology of his time (sometimes elaborate, yet mechanical machines like clockworks) it is understandable that Descartes was of the view that machines cannot use natural language and cannot engage in conversation, since it is hard to think of mechanical devices that possess the above-mentioned abilities.

Turing addressed Descartes's challenge, and in fact defied Descartes's thesis that machines were not able to display intelligence. Turing considered the (still abstract) Turing machine an instrumentation of the mechanical technology Descartes was mentioning. Turing's famous article 'Computing machinery and intelligence' (1950) begins with the question whether machines can think, but Turing swiftly moves on to say that this is in fact a bad question, a question, as Turing puts it, 'too meaningless to deserve discussion' (Turing, 1950: 433). Alternatively, Turing substituted the original question with the question of whether computers can use language. This question refers to the possibility that the micro-operations of calculation add up to something that is – or is indistinguishable from – an actual conversation between, for example, a human being and a machine. In his article, Turing provocatively states that intelligence can be evinced by machines, and developed a test with which one could assess (machine) intelligence. Turing's test involves three actors, a computer actor A, a human actor B and a human actor C (called the 'interrogator'). A, B and C cannot see one another, and are merely able to communicate using a chat-like communication service. The interrogator C does not know which one of the actors A and B is the human actor, and A and B are both instructed to make C think she or he/it is the human actor (i.e. the machine actor is programmed to fool or deceive the interrogator.) Using communication and dialogue, C has to figure out which one of the actors A and B is the human one, and which one is the computer. If the interrogator is not able to pick out which of A and B is human, the computer is said to be 'intelligent'.[10] So, with the test, Turing operationalized the question 'can machines think' with '[c]an machines communicate in natural language in a manner indistinguishable from that of a human being' (Turing, 1950: 434). Turing himself claimed in his 1950 article that he 'believe[d] that by the end of the century, the use of words and general educated opinion will have altered so much that one will be able to speak of machines thinking without expecting to be contradicted' (Turing, 1950: 442). Herbert Simon (2001: 23) stated that intelligence in essence is computation and that a physical symbol system (like a computer) 'has the necessary and sufficient means for general intelligent action'.

Case vignette 2.3: The Loebner Prize

Turing presented the Turing test as a thought experiment, but it should be noted that since 1990, there has been an annual competition called the Loebner Prize.[11] The Loebner Prize (named after its sponsor, the New York philanthropist Hugh Loebner) consists of $100,000 and a gold medal for the first computer whose responses are indistinguishable from a human's responses. Each year, a bronze medal is awarded for the 'most human' achievement. Until now, the gold medal has not been awarded to any participant in the competition. Richard Purtill, author of another *Mind* article, promised to eat his computer library if anyone uncovers the principles to build a machine that can pass the Turing test (Purtill, 1971; Saygin et al., 2000).

Nowadays, so-called chatroom bots are available for use by anyone. Essentially, chatroom bots are software agents (tiny programs) that are programmed to act like participants in chatrooms on the Internet.[12]

Objections to the Turing test

The Turing test – probably best understood as a simple test of thinking that ignores relentless discussion on human nature – has been debated fiercely in past decades (Saygin et al., 2000). Parts of these discussions are insightful because of their conceptualizations of what intelligence is and how it relates to machine intelligence. But there remain just the sort of definitional haggling and interminable arguing that Turing was hoping to put an end to with his test. For example, a number of these arguments have to do with situations in which machines fail to pass the Turing test. According to Turing, failing the Turing test is not to be confused with lack of intelligence. The Turing test is a one-way test: failing it proves nothing, but passing it is a proof for intelligence. Another example of these discussions relates to the question whether intelligence requires *thinking like a human* – in fact, this is not what the Turing test requires. It is the ability of a machine to emulate verbal behaviour, which makes the machine intelligent. In the words of the philosopher Daniel Dennett: if a machine can think in one's own peculiar style well enough to imitate a thinking man or woman, it can think well, indeed.

Turing himself scarcely reflected on the notion of human intelligence. Throughout his career, and in various papers, he reflected on what human intelligence could distinguish from automated reasoning. He came up with properties like 'taking initiative' and 'creativity', and reflected on possibilities to implement these characteristics in terms of symbol manipulation that could be carried out by computers (Hodges, 2000). Turing suggested various possibilities, all based on properties of human brains: learning, teaching, training and searching.[13] According to Turing, the question of whether machines can display intelligence can be reduced to the question of whether initiative and creativity can be taught, learned, trained, and sought for, by general-purpose mechanisms. In the literature, the Turing test is still fiercely debated in the disciplines of information systems, cognitive sciences and psychology. Below, I group a number of arguments that have been used in various debates.

Head in the Sand argument

This objection is the one with the least philosophical or mathematical weight. Some people simply refuse to accept the idea that machines can display intelligence. They argue that notions of cognition, consciousness and machine intelligence simply raise too many questions and so they choose to ignore even the theoretical or hypothetical possibility of the existence of machine intelligence.

Practical Limitations argument

Even if machine intelligence could exist, some authors claim it would require an enormous, unimaginable computing capacity to be meaningfully applied for actual, rather than toy, problems and decision making. Lindblom, for example, wrote the following about the meaning of computers for public administration:

> Yet it is easy to find puzzles and games, some of them simple to arrange, that go beyond the capacity of any man's mind to solve synoptically. Nor can they always be solved synoptically with the help of electronic computers. A.L. Samuals checkers-playing machine would require 10^{21} centuries, supposing that it worked as fast as the fastest imaginable computer, to explore every possible path leading to the end of a game of checkers.
>
> (Baybrooke and Lindblom, 1963: 49)

Mathematical Limitations argument

The mathematician and physicist Roger Penrose stated that every machine (including Turing machines) has fundamental limitations *that do not apply to human beings*. Penrose uses the theorem of the Czech-born mathematician Kurt Gödel. The Gödel theorem states that within any given branch of mathematics, there would always be some propositions that couldn't be proven either true or false using the rules and axioms of that mathematical branch itself.[14] You might be able to prove every conceivable statement about numbers within a system by going *outside* the system in order to come up with new rules and axioms, but by doing so you'll only create a larger system with its own unprovable statements. The implication is that *all* logical systems of any complexity are, by definition, incomplete; each of them contains, at any given time, more true statements than it can possibly prove according to its own defining set of rules. Consequently, a computer can never be as smart as a human being because the extent of its knowledge is limited by a fixed set of axioms, whereas people can discover unexpected truths.

Consciousness argument

Some critics argue that what Turing did when he presented the Turing test was to replace the informal question 'can machines think?' with the somewhat more precise question 'can a digital computer pass a Turing test?' They argue that he did this without reflecting on the notion of intelligence. In fact, in this counterargument, it is stressed that the Turing test does not test intelligence (cognition) but verbal behaviour or linguistic skills (Shieber, 2004). The question is whether a machine that (to an observer) appears to show intelligence, is *conscious* of what it is doing.[15] This argument was previously developed more fully by John Searle (1980), who proposed a variant of the Turing test, called the 'Chinese Room' experiment. In this thought experiment, a native Chinese interrogator asks questions (in Chinese) to a person in a disclosed room who does not know Chinese, but does have an instruction book that tells him how to manipulate certain symbols that are presented to him by the interrogator. The output is sent back to the interrogator. If the interrogator believes that the person with whom he is corresponding understands Chinese, it passes the Turing test but it is obvious that the person in the room does not understand what he is doing and therefore does not display true intelligence. Searle concluded that computers possess syntax, but no semantics (Searle, 1984).

Reflection on the Turing test and on machine intelligence

The Turing test adopts a strong, mainly philosophical criterion of intelligence. The core of the reasoning of Turing seems to be that if a machine can emulate the linguistic and cognitive skills that are needed to engage in a conversation with a human being, it can be regarded as intelligent.[16] Most observers and critics accept that the Turing test is a test of intelligence, and that perhaps in the future computers will be able to pass the test. However alienating and disturbing this conclusion is to some people, there is of course the puzzling question whether machines that pass the Turing test really think, and possess consciousness. As we have seen, Turing and later on Dennett claimed that if computation (symbol manipulation by machines) results in linguistic and cognitive skills that are indistinguishable from human linguistic skills, there is a strong argument for assuming that machines are (or can be) intelligent. Searle, on the other hand, claims that even machines that are capable of passing the Turing test cannot be assumed to possess consciousness.

One answer to these puzzling and highly philosophical questions is that the Turing test assesses whether a machine can *display* intelligence, rather than whether a machine *is* intelligent. This distinction resembles the discrepancies in linguistics and psychology, as presented in the debate between Noam Chomsky and Burrhus Skinner, and between intention and extension; for example is the intentional way in which a result is obtained more important than the extensional result? As the Turing test is more concerned with the extensional way of testing intelligence, the test itself cannot be used to really shed light on matters of the nature of human intelligence, or consciousness. Indeed, Alan Turing never wanted to enter into these discussions.

In the above discussions, reflections on cognition, intelligence and consciousness have been presented. Most articles and books that address the Turing test use psychology, philosophy or computer sciences as angles for analysis and reflection. In doing do, some of the psychological and philosophical questions regarding *smart machines* have been addressed. However, these psychological and philosophical questions pertain to the level of individuals, thus ignoring the social context in which ICTs are implemented, and the real world 'out there'. In these debates, the question whether computers can add to organizational or policy learning, remains unanswered. This issue is briefly addressed by Benny Shannon (1989) who claims that intelligence is also embedded in social processes, and thus should also be analysed at a collective (as opposed to an individual) level. An attempt to pay attention to the social context is Barresi's Cyberiad Test, this is passed if 'a society of artificial men are able to continue a socio-cultural evolution of their own without disintegration' (Barresi, 1987: 23). However, in the theory and practice of public administration, the social (organizational, macro-societal) context necessitates more attention to social aspects of intelligence than Barresi does. In order to address these issues, I first turn to *functional* characteristics of existing ICTs in the practice of public administration. After enumerating these characteristics, attention will be paid to questions of how machine intelligence relates to organizational contexts and societal, democratic contexts.

Characteristics of existing ICTs

Functional characteristics of smart machines

While the basic characteristics define core operations of computers, they do not delineate actual *uses* or *functions* at a more pragmatic, practical level. Of course, as has been indicated above, computers are able to perform calculations, and indeed the first uses of computers that have taken place in the fields of public administration were uses in which the ability to perform calculations was crucial (ballistics in the military domain, economic modelling, census). Bekkers (1994) identified some more generalized functional characteristics of smart machines. These functional characteristics (which stem from the basic, defining characteristics of smart machines) are elaborated below.

Functional characteristic 1: processing transactions

Transactions are series of operations or sub-operations performed upon data, with the results being communicated to external partners. An example of a transaction is the payment of an allowance (which has been decided upon in an automated fashion) to a beneficiary. Given automated rules (algorithms) that formalize who is entitled to receive allowances (or, inversely, what penalties should be given as a result of specific forms of deviant behaviour like speeding), or data describing the circumstances that are relevant, computers can process enormous amounts of information. This also applies to the application of formalized rules in other areas with other examples including the levying of taxes, study grants, allowances, permit handling and so on. Of course, in order for machines to process transactions, rules must be formalized into algorithms that conclusively state what kinds of antecedents result in specific legal (or financial) consequences.

Functional characteristic 2: control and discipline

ICTs can also monitor, control and discipline. This enables governments to guide behaviour of individual citizens. An example can be found in the electronic facilities of tax agencies (websites) that enable the electronic submission of facts and figures by citizens and corporations. On the one hand, the existence of these facilities can be interpreted as a move towards client-orientation and responsive public service delivery; on the other hand, these websites provide rather compelling procedures and guidelines on how, when and in what format citizens have to comply with the general requirements of submitting information. On the basis of gathered historical information on the prevalence of fraud in specific target populations, tax agencies can decide to electronically monitor (and thoroughly check submissions by) specific target groups more tightly than others (see also Zouridis, 2000).

The use of traffic monitoring systems provides another example of how smart machines enable regional traffic authorities to oversee the activities of citizens. By means of monitoring traffic, traffic authorities can impose speed limits and, hypothetically, even automatically sanction speeding without any form of human intervention or judgement. During the 2001 Super Bowl sport events in the United States, law enforcement agencies used pattern-matching software to compare video stills of spectators with photos from criminal records. This makes it possible to localize and track down known, convicted criminals on the loose.[17]

Functional characteristic 3: generating transparency

Computers – through the basic, defining characteristic of 'memory', allow for greater levels of transparency – both transparency of the administrative apparatus, as well as transparency of societal sectors.

With respect to transparency of the administrative apparatus, Meijer (2002) concluded that the use of smart machines in public administration allows for more and better parliamentary, public and legal scrutiny of administrative and political behaviour. In general, external scrutiny of affairs by Administrative Courts, Ombudsmen and Parliamentary Committees is greatly enhanced by the availability of huge amounts of data. This gives rise to the concept of the 'transparent state' (Meijer, 2002). Meijer gives the example of the Tower Committee that investigated the Irangate-Contras Affair in the United States. Crucial in the investigation was the email correspondence of Oliver North (National Security Council) and National Security Adviser John Poindexter. Although both North and Poindexter deleted potentially compromising email messages from servers, the messages were recovered and handed over to the committee for further use in the investigations (Blanton, 1995). More generally, we also witness the increased availability of information on public performance and public expenditure to the general public. In the United States, and to a lesser degree in the European Union, there has been a long-standing tradition of emphasizing the importance of access to so-called public sector information (Aichholzer and Burkert, 2004). In the United States, the Freedom of Information Act requires federal agencies to disclose records as they are requested (in writing) by any citizen.[18] The Freedom of Information Act has existed for a very long time, but the potential of 'public sector transparency' is greatly enhanced by smart machines' 'memory' capabilities. In the Netherlands, several quasi-autonomous agencies voluntarily report on their performance to the general public by publishing performance information on their websites (Schillemans, 2005). Of course these developments are hardly caused by the emergence of ICTs, but in general it can be said that administrative transparency or the transparent state is in fact enabled by the availability of modern technologies like the Internet. At least it makes it much easier not only for public sector organizations to disclose and proactively publish public sector information but also for citizens to access public sector information.

Aside from administrative transparency (transparency of the administrative apparatus, in the eyes of the general public), ICTs also enable an inverse form of transparency, namely the transparency of society in the eyes of government. For instance, Power (1997) noted an increase in auditing activity in the United Kingdom and North America. He wrote, 'The growth of auditing is the explosion of an idea, an idea that has become central to a certain style of controlling individuals and which has permeated organizational life' (Power, 1997: 4). This explosion of auditing activity can, for instance, be witnessed in the form of a rapid growth in the number of international *policy monitors* (Mayne and Zapico-Goni, 1997). Monitoring is the systematic and periodic description of societal developments by public administration. The increase in the number of policy monitors used in administrative practice is stimulated by the availability of ICTs since they enable the processing of massive amounts of information. The rise of monitoring as a trend is an indicator of increasing levels of societal transparency, with which administrations and politicians attempt to control the course of implementing policy proposals (De Kool and Van Buren, 2004). This can be with the goal of adjusting implementation strategies to improve realization of public policy goals more generally.

Functional characteristic 4: communication

A significant development in the availability and spread of computing power is the rise of telecommunication technology and the subsequent popularity of computer networking. Basically, computer networking relates to the access by a specific computer of information that is stored on another computer. Examples include searching library databases (which are probably stored at one of the library's servers) from your personal computer at home, or accessing your bank account using the Internet. Of course the Internet itself is the most vivid example of computer networking: while browsing the web, you are accessing web pages and other information resources that are stored on distinct web servers in Brazil, Indonesia, the Fiji Islands, and so forth. While sending mails, you are sending messages to mail servers that are somewhere on the Internet.

The basic idea of networking, in the form of the Internet as we know it today, emerged in the late 1950s in the United States. President Eisenhower directed the Defence Department to establish a telecommunication network (ARPA: Advanced Research Projects Agency) which was to be used for supporting military research. It was designed to be very robust since the network had to be able to continue to function even when some parts (or nodes) of the network were under attack. In particular, the network was to be designed and implemented in such a way that it could remain operational even after a number of components had been destroyed, for example by means of nuclear attacks. In order to conform to this design requirement, the ARPA network incorporated a high degree of redundancy, *packet switching* was implemented. Packet switching is a technique in which messages (which are basically sequences of bits) to be transferred over networks are not transmitted as a fixed sequence, the message is separated into a number of packets, with each packet being addressed to the receiver, and headed for instructions for reassembly once it has reached its destination. Each packet is also instructed to follow the most efficient possible route across a distributed network. If, upon arrival, it is clear that a packet is missing, the receiving processor sends a request to the originating processor, which dispatches a 'twin'-packet. Although the above explanation of packet switching is overly simplistic (an adequate technical explanation of the workings of packet switching stretches beyond the scope of this book), it should be stressed that with the technique of packet switching, a solution was found to communicate messages in distributed environments, and enabling packets to be relatively invulnerable to breakdowns of the network. For instance, if one possible route is busy or malfunctioning, packets simply avoid the obstruction and proceed to the destination using another route. This concept turned out to be very fruitful for long-distance communication, and the concept of packet switching attracted attention outside the military realm in which it was developed. Slowly, the ARPA network grew out of the military environment in which it had originated, into the academic realm. Much to the surprise of ARPA developers, by 1973, it was found that 75 per cent of all ARPA network traffic consisted of a semiformal, a barely allowed form of communication or rather email messages.

By 1972, packet switching networks were being developed throughout the world and, more importantly, they were increasingly being connected. In 1983, the computer scientists' CSNET was connected to the Canadian CA*net, and later on to BITNET, Usenet (a network for users of Unix systems, which grew out to be a distributed network of newsgroups) and FidoNet (Barney, 2000). Gradually, a network of networks emerged that is now known by the name of Internet.

A specific application on the Internet, the World Wide Web, grew out of Internet technology when Tim Berners-Lee of the European Nuclear Research Centre developed the idea of hyperlinks in 1992. Tim Berners-Lee thought of a concept with which he could easily access documents available at servers, and developed the idea of URL addresses (implemented in hyperlinks). By referring to documents with the location on the server where they originate (for example, http://www.eur.nl, a so-called Uniform Resource Locator) he could easily access resources. The concept of URLs (in various categories, for text-based documents, sounds, images, movies) gave way to a graphic, multimedia environment which we nowadays refer to as the World Wide Web.

The rise of email communication, chat services and increased use of third (and in the near future, fourth) generation cell phones,[19] to name just a few examples, mark an entirely different function of computers. In general they allow for communication between individuals regardless of where the individuals are located. This is provided that they are 'wired' or wirelessly connected to computer networks, and assuming that asynchronous communication facilities, like electronic mail accounts and discussion boards, do not require individuals to respond to one another at the same moment in time.

In public administration, information is increasingly exchanged through email correspondence (Meijer, 2005). Edwards (2005) noted that electronic communication facilities, moreover, enabled new forms of political communication among politicians, journalists, concerned citizens and representatives of interest organizations. New forms of communication in these so-called 'cybermediaries' allow for institutional innovation and democratic renewal.

Functional characteristic 5: virtual reality

A final functional characteristic is *virtual reality*. By means of combining data from various sources, combining and selecting data, and graphic representation of data sets in real-life environments, real-life environments can be simulated. This can enable the consequences of alternative policy solutions, for example, to be visualized. At this time, there are ample applications in the field of spatial planning (Onsrud, 2007).

Machine intelligence and organizational context

Intelligence in a social context

So what does the prospect of genuinely smart machines – if they will ever be built – mean for government organizations and for the ways in which policies are developed and implemented? Do smart machines make organizations smarter, and are there avenues for smarter public governance and smarter democracies? If the micro-operations of symbol manipulation indeed add up to intelligence, one might assume they do. But even if one takes this view, one might still question whether computers in the real world of democratic societies and organizations – that is, not in mind games and thought experiments – contribute to intelligent decision making and intelligent social behaviour. What happens, however, if we apply our social shaping of technology (SST) perspective and analyse interactions of possibly smart machines with the contexts in which they are applied and implemented? In general, quite opposing views exist. One optimistic view is that computers enable the widespread availability of information and knowledge in society, and contribute to greater freedom and greater incentive to concentrate on what is fully human, and rehumanize the images of ourselves (Boden, 1990). Boden argues that as such, computers could revolutionize our capacity for creativity and problem solving, much as the invention of printing did. A pessimistic view, on the other hand, results from scenarios in which totalitarian states use computers to gather all kind of information about individuals, thereby threatening privacy and creating a Big Brother.

Eventual effects depend not only on the type of information and communication technology that is implemented, but also on the type of context in which the technology is used. It involves trade-offs and the confrontation of various values. Therefore, I devote attention below to some of the authors that have contributed to the understanding of ways in which information and communication technologies can contribute to or, inversely, decrease intelligence in a true social (organizational or societal) context.

Intelligence in an organizational context: Zuboff's informating capacities

The relationship between *smart machines* and organizations has been analysed by, among many others, Shoshana Zuboff (1988). Her book does not address the question what makes a machine 'smart' or 'intelligent', but rather asks how (and in whose interest) technologies would be used in an organizational context. Furthermore, she addresses the question how smart machines would affect the human factor (including notions of learning, reflection and intelligence) in organizations.

Zuboff's assumption is that information and communication technologies are comparable to mechanical devices in the sense that both types of technologies can be used for *automation* (the substitution of human activities with automated activities). ICTs are qualitatively different from mechanical technologies, however, because of their specific ability to *informate*. By *informating*, Zuboff means the abilities of information and communication technologies to 'register data about ... automated activities, thus generating new streams of information' (Zuboff, 1988: 9). This view of informating is echoed by Michael Scott-Morton (1991) in his 'Management of the 1990s' programme:

> Information technology has important general-purpose power to manipulate symbols used in all classes of work, and therefore, as an 'information

engine', it can do for business what the steam engine did in the days of the Industrial Revolution. It goes beyond this, however, as a technology that permits one to manipulate models of reality, to step back one pace from the physical reality. Such an ability lies at the heart of IT's capacity to alter work fundamentally.

(Scott-Morton, 1991: 8)

Thus ICTs are able to create a detailed kind of informational mirror of all kinds of physical activities and transactions in and surrounding organizations. 'Information technology not only produces action but also produces a voice that symbolically renders events, objects and processes so that they become visible, knowable and sharable in every way' (Zuboff, 1988: 9). ICTs therefore enable the automation of processes, as well as enabling them to be displayed as data. As a consequence, it is argued, ICTs are able to make organizations more transparent than previously.

To grasp the forces behind, and consequences of, automating and informating, Zuboff (1988) describes a complicated organizational reality, consisting of both *intrinsic* as well as *sinister* consequences.

With *intrinsic* consequences, Zuboff (1988) denotes the increased insight yielded to all employees through informating. If all employees are allowed by management to exercise greater critical judgement in applying technology to tasks, this will promote new forms of intellectual skills, meaning, and opportunity that can come to pervade organizations. In other words: technology may enable and entice employees to develop more intellective skills, to reflect on their own behaviour, to share information more generously, and develop ways to interact and collaborate. With *intrinsic* consequences Zuboff refers to employees working in organizations that actually have access to the informational image through smart machines. She envisages employees interpreting the informational image and deploying more intelligent human thought and action, as a result of the enhanced learning of all levels of employees, including the lower levels.

On the other hand, there are *sinister* consequences. Zuboff argues that with the above-mentioned enhanced learning capacities of lower levels of staff, traditional authority exercised by higher levels of staff (i.e., management) is contested: 'The informating process sets knowledge and authority on a collision course' (Zuboff, 1988: 310). Zuboff describes situations in which smart machines are used to generate a so-called *information panopticon*. A panopticon is an architectural concept used to exercise control by observers (watchmen, guards and the like) over those who had escaped social forms of authority, such as inmates, convicts and paupers. It consisted of a tower in which the observers resided, as well as separate cells in which inhabitants dwelled. A system of mirrors in the form of a polygon was used in the panopticon to enable observers to monitor inhabitants of cells, while the inhabitants were unable to see the observer. The construction of the tower, the system of mirrors and the cells, provided for 'universal transparency'. This means that the panopticon, and its characteristic illumination and visibility, provided observers the possibility of total control over inhabitants.

Total control emerged not only from actual monitoring of behaviour, but also from the psychological effect that inhabitants did not know exactly when they were being monitored and when they were not. As Zuboff notes, the psychological effects of visibility alone, as opposed to the effects of actually being monitored, are enough to ensure appropriate conduct and compliant behaviour. The idea of a panopticon (which was coined by Jeremy Bentham and discussed in the British Parliament in the eighteenth century as a possible solution to the problems of observation and control in prisons) inspired Michel Foucault to speak of panopticism as a principle of strengthening relations of discipline and control, and that can be used to impose particular forms of behaviour. An information panopticon is a form of surveillance (or, as Zuboff calls it, *dataveillance*) with which continuously, hard, supposedly objective data from primary processes is recorded for the purpose of controlling, disciplining and possibly sanctioning shirking by lower-level employees. In this way, smart machines are being used as panoptical devices that enshrine control in data, thus destroying initiative and creativity of workers, and decreasing organizational intelligence with it. To this extent human intelligence could, according to Zuboff, make way for machine intelligence.

What we see here is that technologies can be conceived of as Janus-faced concepts. They can produce completely opposing consequences depending on the organizational or general social contexts in which they are put to use and, as illustrated above, the degree to which employees at specific levels are granted access to information generated by smart machines. Walton (1989) refers to this effect as the dual organizational potentialities of ICTs.

Case vignette 2.4: Better tools, better workers

David Haines (2003) described how application of ICTs in a US state workers' compensation agency resulted in significant improvements in the agency's work. Haines focuses on the introduction of a set of applications for verifying that employers had workers' compensation insurance. At the end of the 1980s, a mainframe system administered by a separate agency was replaced by a dedicated database system. As a result, employees and management experienced increased autonomy (as compared to the old situation), enabling them to communicate in other ways, to expand the system in new areas, and to find creative ways of carrying out tasks (Haines, 2003). As many laborious tasks could be automated, employees changed from being production workers (writing repetitive letters, manually cross-checking data) to supervisors of production processes. As a consequence, they had more oversight over production processes and workers had become, at least partly, a contact for employers or employees with specific questions and compensation insurance. Haines concludes that

> as machine competence transformed staff into supervisors – labor into management – it would begin to dissolve hierarchical relationships.

Furthermore, as work became increasingly visible, it would become increasingly self-monitoring. Everybody would know what everybody else was doing, and the logic of much line management would disappear.

(Haines, 2003: 465)

Although there are caveats to the story – the difficulties for 'traditional' management to cope with the new situation, the question of how to deal with superfluous labour force – Haines' account makes clear how the introduction of information and communication technologies can result in new lateral alignment between technology, labour and management, and how other interactions between humans and computers (de-physicalizing the relation between work and data) eventually resulted in the emergence of teams. The emergence of teams could not be explained out of managerial direction, but rather emerged out of newly created patterns of how work was actually done.

One of the major insights from Zuboff is the clarification of the processes of *deskilling* and *re-skilling* that occurs as a result of the implementation of ICTs. The direct connection of people with production processes is eliminated, and action-centred skills are replaced with intellective skills involving the interpretation of abstract symbols remote from physical reality (Jaffee, 2001). This, according to Zuboff, will not automatically make organizations as a whole smarter. It depends upon the training and nurturing of intellective skills in organizations and the opportunity to exercise and perform these skills (Jaffee, 2001). Whether ICTs make organizations smarter or more intelligent is therefore not dependent upon the properties of information and communication technologies alone.

Machine intelligence and democracy

In the previous section, the notion and effects of smart machines in an organizational context have been analysed. For the discipline of public administration, it has also been intriguing to ask the question whether ICTs can contribute to more intelligent forms of policy making, or an intelligent democracy.

In general, the emergence of ICTs has led so-called techno-optimists to herald the *rationalization* of politics and democracy (Dror, 1964). In this view, policy making and policy processes are generally seen as cumbersome, overly prone to inertia and susceptible to effects of the cognitive limits of decision makers. ICTs, however, can (and in this view should) allow for more rational governance. ICTs can be used to gather more information from society and identify more policy alternatives. Through the use of simulation models and policy analysis methods, they are able to identify more accurately the consequences of various policy alternatives. For techno-optimists ICTs open up avenues for a *synoptic ideal of policy making*: it pushes policy making towards a *central rule approach* (van Gunsteren, 1976), in which their use by policy makers enables better informed, increasingly balanced and fast-paced decision making. Perri 6 describes how techno-optimists presented ICTs as solutions with which ambiguity and uncertainty could be eliminated (6, 2004). He furthermore describes how, in the 1980s, politicians began to use spreadsheet software for budget setting in detail, rather than leaving these issues to finance directors and Treasury civil servants.[20]

The flip side of these forms of ICT-enabled rationalization of democratic decision making are highlighted by Van de Donk (1998). His detailed empirical study of Dutch nursing homes found that decision making about budgets took place in an arena in which various administrative groups and societal interest groups employed ICT applications (notably rather simple spreadsheet applications) to contest positions and interests. He concluded:

> The real world of information processing in the domain of public policy making does not at all comply with the claim of a predominantly analytical and systematic use of scientific information. Instead, it is characterized by several types of information ... and information politics.... Information is an important source to reduce all kinds of cognitive and strategic uncertainties and also an important weapon in all kinds of info-politics and *data wars* that time and time again characterize the policy making process.
>
> (Van de Donk, 1998: 391)

Van de Donk also concluded that the application of ICTs in the longer run resulted in stronger administrative hierarchies and favoured unilateral exercise of power by technocrats and technocratic politicians. This would occur at the expense of the participation of a myriad of societal interest groups, whose presence and influence are seen by Van de Donk as indispensable conditions for actual democratic (or, as Van de Donk phrases it, *institutional*) intelligence.

Following Van de Donk (1998), it is possible to claim that rational decision making, which is supposedly favoured by the application of smart machines, does not necessarily lead to more democratic decision making. On the contrary, appealing to an incremental (as opposed to a rational) view on policy making (Lindblom, 1965), Van de Donk (1998) argues that stronger administrative hierarchies lead to a decrease in what he calls 'the intelligence of democracy'. This is because smart machines in policy making processes lead to myopia, rule-bound policy making, decreased plurality and tunnel vision. The essence of an 'intelligent democracy' is that it is open and responsive. Democratic intelligence, in this view, emerges out of interactions between societal groups and out of pluralism. Van de Donk concludes that contemporary applications of smart machines (notably the use of ICTs in redistributive policy making) affects the plurality in society, and with that, the learning capabilities of a democratic society. In this view, smart machines threaten democratic intelligence.

Conclusions

In this chapter, information and communication technologies have been described as possible manifestations of smart machines. These are general purpose machines that are able to manipulate symbols, and have a basic prerequisite for carrying out a huge array of tasks, varying from game playing to computer-aided design, computer integrated manufacturing, weather forecasting, execution of legislation, education and training of specific skills, to name only a few applications.

In the disciplines of philosophy, cognitive sciences and computer science, the possibility that this kind of machines can display intelligence is fiercely debated. I have argued in this chapter that the question is not whether to *believe* in smart machines or not. Rather the issue at stake is to reflect upon what properties could make computers intelligent, what intelligence actually is, and what the prospects and limits are to machine intelligence. The aim of this chapter has been to allow the reader to make an opinion about the role of computers in decision making, social planning and policy (cf. Simon, 2001). Scientists and philosophers like Alan Turing, Herbert Simon and Daniel Dennett claim that if computers are able to master linguistic and cognitive skills indistinguishable from human linguistic and cognitive skills, there is a strong argument for assuming that machines are (or can be) intelligent. Indeed, Herbert Simon has asserted that symbol manipulation, the core activity of computers, is a necessary and sufficient means for intelligent action. There remains, however, the matter of whether thinking machines are conscious of their own thoughts. This has led Searle (1984) to oppose the belief that any computer can display intelligence because machines are not truly aware or conscious of their own thoughts.

If one assumes that computers can display intelligence, then there are avenues for interesting applications in public administration. Some of these have been realized; while others remain in the domain of science fiction. For several years now the execution of legislation has been realized in domains of social security and tax laws. Techno-utopians even foresee that computers in the near future will be able to adequately judge court cases, while present-day engineers and developers have already made progress in embedding at least rudimentary forms of intelligence in computer systems.

The point that has been made in this chapter is that these systems do not of themselves ensure that horizons are opened for a more social connotation of intelligence. It has been shown that although computer systems are more or less intelligent at a cognitive level, and possibly have some characteristics of initiative and creativity, they do not necessarily contribute to intelligent behaviour in social and political contexts. When computers are implemented in real world situations, rather than the thought experiments that were the habitats of the discussions about machine intelligence and smart machines, several scenarios can be envisaged. These depend upon the type of computer technology that is implemented, the characteristics of the social environment in which the technology is applied, and the value and norms (about, for example, democracy) that prevail in specific environments. The intelligence of organizations and the intelligence of democracy, to paraphrase and reiterate Lindblom (1965), is definitely not solely about computation, but also about fostering other kinds rationalism. The emergence of smart machines in the world of public administration therefore focuses attention on institutional context, and not only on matters of cognition and consciousness of smart machines. Whether computation and symbol manipulation eventually result in intelligence of organization, policy and democracy remains therefore an open question.

Discussion questions

1   Name and discuss various arguments in favour of and opposing the use of ICTs in the execution of policy (for example, ICTs that issue administrative orders in the field of environmental law).
2   Name and discuss various arguments in favour of and opposing the use of ICTs in court ordering (for example, ICTs that issue sanctions in relation to speeding or financial fraud).
3   Describe and elaborate on the issue of 'spreadsheet politics'. In what circumstances is 'spreadsheet politics' likely to occur?
4   In the discussion of Zuboff's vision on organizational intelligence, a distinction was made between intrinsic and sinister consequences. In what circumstances do you think either intrinsic or sinister consequences will prevail?
5   Rationalists like Dror have argued that ICTs enable rationalization of decision making processes, and political behaviour in general. What circumstances or characteristics prohibit rationalization, according to commentators opposing Dror's view?

Notes

1   Note the character of the seducing robot Maria, who was created by the inventor Rotwang in Fritz Lang's 1927 movie *Metropolis*, and the robot characters in Isaac Asimov's novels.
2   This is according to the assumptions of endless tape and infinite memory. Turing also proved that there are problems the Turing machine cannot solve, and hence these problems cannot be solved by any digital computer.
3   Digital here means that the machine has access to a finite number of internal states only. Analogue machines have access, in principle, to an infinite number of internal states and could therefore be expected to outperform digital machines.
4   Note that there is a finite set of symbols, for example {0,1, *} where '*' denotes a stop instruction.
5   During the Second World War, the US Army (Ballistics Research Laboratory) further developed the Colossus design and built the Electronic Numerical Integrator And Computer (ENIAC), which was used for the purpose of calculating ballistic firing tables.
6   Hodges (2000) points at parallel developments in psychology, such as neural physiology and behaviourism.

7 For a more elaborate description of Alan Turing's work, refer to www.turing.org.uk (last visited 9 February 2006).
8 All that is required are the general Boolean operations AND, OR and NOT. For the sake of brevity, the mathematic origins of Boolean logic are not explained here.
9 http://blogs.business2.com/utilitybelt/2007/09/live-moira-gunn.html (last visited 21 September 2007).
10 There has been much debate over the question whether the Turing test is a necessary or a sufficient condition for thought.
11 See http://www.loebner.net/Prizef/loebner-prize.html (last visited 10 September 2007).
12 See for example http://www.alicebot.org/ (last visited 21 September 2007).
13 Learning in the context of Turing machines relates to possibilities for machines to alter their algorithms or programs. These kinds of algorithms, coined genetic algorithms, were proposed by Richard Friedberg in 1958.
14 A well-known example is the statement 'This statement is NOT true'. This statement can never be disproven: the statement-as-it-is-stated may be true but, because the statement is not true, it is not (so it is false and contradicts the statement-as-it-is-stated). By means of reflection, humans are able to spot the self-referential character of the statement, yet machines are not able to do so.
15 One position here is that although the language uttered by a machine may persuade observers to think a machine is human, it is produced by another internal 'mechanism' than the human brain and hence the machine is not intelligent. Another position is that any artefact that is capable of complex sorts of linguistic behaviour is indeed communicating in language and not merely appearing to, and hence can be regarded as intelligent.
16 The Turing test thus tests for human-like intelligence. It is therefore sometimes called anthropomorphic.
17 http://news.bbc.co.uk/1/hi/sci/tech/1500017.stm (last visited 21 September 2007).
18 Agencies may withhold information pursuant to nine exemptions; these exemptions refer to situations in which national security is at stake, or requested information refers to trade secrets, law enforcement files, personal data and pre-decisional documents.
19 Fourth generation cell phones are mobile phones with which users can be simultaneously connected to one another using multiple wireless access technologies such as EDGE, UMTS and WiFi.
20 Dutch Minister of Social Affairs and Employment, Bert de Vries (in power from 1989 to 1994) was known for his competences to master spreadsheet software by himself to check and verify calculations made by tens of members of specialist staff.

References

6, P. (2004). *E-Governance: Styles of Political Judgement in the Information Age Polity.* Basingstoke: Palgrave Macmillan.

Aichholzer, G., and Burkert, H. (eds) (2004). *Public Sector Information in the Digital Age.* Cheltenham: Edward Elgar.

Augarten, S. (1984). *BIT by BIT: An Illustrated History of Computers.* New York: Ticknor and Fields.

Barney, D. (2000). *Promotheus Wired: The Hope for Democracy in the Age of Network Technology.* Chicago, IL: University of Chicago Press.

Barresi, J. (1987). Prospects for the cyberiad: Certain limits on human self knowledge in the Cybernetic Age. *Journal for the Theory of Social Behaviour, 17,* 19–46.

Baybrooke, D., and Lindblom, C. (1963). *A Strategy of Decision: Policy Evaluation as a Social Process.* New York: The Free Press.

Bekkers, V. J. J. M. (1994). *Nieuwe vormen van sturing en informatisering (New Forms of Steering and Informating)*. Delft: Eburon.

Blanton, T. (ed.) (1995). *White House Email: The Top Secret Messages the Reagan/Bush White House Tried to Destroy*. New York: The Free Press.

Boden, M. (1990). The age of intelligent machines: The social impact of artificial intelligence. In R. Kurzweil (ed.) *The Age of Intelligent Machines*. Cambridge, MA: MIT Press.

Clarke, R. (1993). Asimov's Laws of Robotics: Implications for information technology. Part 1. *Computer, 26*(12), 53–61.

Clarke, R. (1994). Asimov's Laws of Robotics. Implications for Information Technology. Part 2. *Computer, 27*(1), 57–68.

De Kool, D., and Van Buren, A. (2004). Monitoring: Functional or fashionable? *Economy and Society, 26*(2–3), 173–193.

Descartes, R. (1637/1985). Discourse on method. In J. Cottingham, R. Stoothoff and D. Murdoch (eds) *The Philosophical Writings of Descartes*. Cambridge: Cambridge University Press.

Dror, Y. (1964). Muddling through: 'Science' or inertia. *Public Administration Review, 24*, 153–157.

Edwards, A. (2005). Niches for new intermediairies. In V. J. J. M. Bekkers and V. M. F. Homburg (eds) *The Information Ecology of E-Government (E-Government as Institutional and Technological Innovation in Public Administration)*. Amsterdam: IOS Press.

Haines, D. (2003). Better tools, better workers: Toward a lateral aligment of technology, policy, labour and management. *American Review of Public Administration, 33*(4), 449–478.

Hirose, S. (1996). A code of conduct for robots coexisting with human beings. *Robotics and Autonomous Systems, 18*(1–2), 101–107.

Hodges, A. (2000). Turing, a natural philosopher. In R. Monk and F. Raphael (eds) *The Great Philosophers*. London: Weidenfeld and Nicolson.

Jaffee, D. (2001). *Organization Theory: Tension and Change*. New York: McGraw-Hill.

Lindblom, C. (1965). *The Intelligence of Democracy: Decision Making through Mutual Adjustment*. New York: The Free Press.

Mayne, J. M., and Zapico-Goni, E. (eds) (1997). *Monitoring Performance in the Public Sector: Future Directions From International Experience*. New Brunswick, NJ: Transaction.

Meijer, A. (2002). *De doorzichtige overheid (Parlementaire en juridische controle in het informatietijdperk)*. Delft: Eburon.

Meijer, A. (2005). Email in government: Networks in the shadow of hierarchy. In M. Khosrow-Pour (ed.) *Managing Modern Organizations with Information Technology*. Hershey, PA: Idea Group.

Onsrud, H. (ed.) (2007). *Research and Theory in Advancing Spatial Data Infrastructure Concepts*. Redlands, CA: ESRI Press.

Power, M. (1997). *The Audit Society*. Oxford: Oxford University Press.

Purtill, R. L. (1971). Beating the imitation game. *Mind, 80*, 290–294.

Saygin, A. P., Cecekli, I., and Akman, V. (2000). Turing test: 50 years later. *Minds and Machines, 10*, 463–518.

Schillemans, T. (2005). Verantwoording na verzelfstandiging. Continuïteit, vernieuwing en verwarring. In W. Bakker and K. Yesilkagit (eds) *Publieke verantwoording: Regimes van inzicht en rekenschap bij de uitvoering van publieke taken*. Amsterdam: Boom.

Scott-Morton, M. S. (1991). *The Corporation of the 1990s*. New York: Oxford University Press.

Searle, J. R. (1980). Minds, brains and programs. *Behavioural and Brain Sciences, 1*, 417–424.

Searle, J. R. (1984). *Minds, Brains and Science*. London: BBS Press.

Shannon, B. (1989). A simple comment regarding the Turing test. *Journal for the Theory of Social Behavior, 19*(2), 249–256.

Shieber, S. (2004). *The Turing test: Verbal Behaviour as the Hallmark of Intelligence*. Cambridge, MA: MIT Press.

Simon, H. (2001). *The Sciences of the Artificial*. Cambridge, MA: MIT Press.

Turing, A. (1950). Computing machinery and intelligence. *Mind, 59*, 433–460.

Van de Donk, W. B. H. J. (1998). Beyond incrementalism? Redistributive policy making, information systems and revival of synopticism. In I. T. M. Snellen (ed.) *Public Administration in an Information Age*. Amsterdam: IOS Press.

van den Herik, J. (1991). *Kunnen computers rechtspreken?* Arnhem: Gouda Quint.

van Gunsteren, H. R. (1976). *The Quest for Control*. London: Wiley.

Walton, R. E. (1989). *Up and Running: Integrating Information Technology and the Organization*. Boston, MA: Harvard University Press.

Weizenbaum, J. (1979). *Computer Power and Human Reason*. New York: The Free Press.

Zouridis, S. (2000). *Digitale disciplinering: over ICT, organisatie, wetgeving en het automatiseren van beschikkingen*. Tilburg: Katholieke Universiteit Brabant.

Zuboff, S. (1988). *In the Age of the Smart Machine: The Future of Work and Power*. New York: Basic Books.

3   The Information Society

Key points

After reading this chapter, you will be able to

- describe and define the 'Information Society'
- describe how the Information Society has emerged as a result from technological, economic, occupational, spatial and cultural developments
- explain how the processes within the Information Society challenge traditional ideas of public policy and the State, and what possible roles are for public authorities in the Information Society.

Introduction

In this book, the intricate relation between public administration and technology is analysed and reflected upon. In Chapter 2, characteristics of contemporary information and communication technologies were presented, and their uses in organizational and democratic practices were discussed. There are, however, numerous authors who argue that the impact and significance of ICTs stretches far beyond the limited scope of public administration and public policy. They claim that ICTs are relevant for changes occurring in the fabric of our society or, in other words, at a macro level. In other words, we are either entering a new era which is called the Information Age (Castells, 1996, 2000), or our society develops into an Information Society or e-society (Lips, 2005; Webster, 2002). Both connotations recognize fundamental differences from respectively previous eras and previous social structure.

One of the leading authors on the Information Society, Manuel Castells, refers to the Information Society as a society in which activities and economic production take place in a technological paradigm, constituted around information and communication technologies.[1] Castells argues that in the Information Society, the focus is not so much on products and services, but rather on an informational mode of production. He conceives of creating, manipulating and distributing information and knowledge as being at the core of our economy. According to Castells, the entrance of information and knowledge production to the centre stage of our economy has the consequence that technological developments result in new forms of social interaction, control and social developments.

It still may be asked what is actually new in the Information Society? Some argue that information and knowledge have always played an important role in explaining the structure of our organizations, especially bureaucratic organizations, and societies. The idea of a fundamentally different Information Society, however, has entered not only the realm of academic spectators and commentators, but also the world of policy makers and politicians who are increasingly speaking about the possible consequences of a globalized, informational economy. In addition, various governments throughout the world have drafted or are in the process of drafting policies that address the challenges and problems of Information Societies. Information Society policies are usually policies that address the development of ICT infrastructures and skills with the intention to stimulate the economy and to prevent digital exclusion of citizens in society (Janssen and Rotthier, 2005).

In this chapter, the Information Society is analysed by scrutinizing the concepts and developments that have been associated with the Information Society by leading authors. The aim is to try to get beneath their concept of the Information Society. Furthermore, the challenges of the Information Society for governments and public administration are explicitly addressed. In order to do that, the first section sketches the contours of the Information Society concept. Paradoxes and challenges of the Information Society are then identified, while the role of government and public administration are discussed in the following section. Finally, conclusions and reflection are presented.

The contours of the Information Society

Introduction

Various authors have written copiously about the role, consequences, place and antecedents of 'information' and 'knowledge' in the society we live in. In fact, the Information Society has been discussed in books and articles since the 1960s (Lips, 2005). In numerous writings, we are increasingly being told we live in an Information Age, Information Society or 'e-Society', with specific mechanisms that drive our economies. We are told that we have moved to a global, networked, interconnected economy that thrives on intangible flows of information and capital that themselves have no relationship with time and place.

It is difficult to come up with one definition that captures all of the relevant features of what is often called the 'Information Society'. Webster (2002) identifies five developments that coincide, and together bring into being a new type of social system, the 'information society'. These five concurrent developments are discussed below.

Technological developments

First, technological innovations in the field of telecommunication technology, such as cable and satellite television or wide-area computer networks, have been particularly significant in descriptions of the Information Society. Since they constitute such an array of innovations nowadays, many authors have argued that they must lead to a reconstitution of the social world because their impact is so profound. Most remarkably, they have provided corporations, governments and non-governmental organizations the possibility (at relatively low costs) to exchange information globally on worldwide technological infrastructures (for instance, the Internet) that allow instant computer communication, 24 hours a day, 7 days a week. Basically, the emergence of information and communication technologies as a series of innovations is seen as a key characteristic of a new era – comparable to the emergence of mechanical technology (steam machines, combustion engines). As Naisbitt phrased it: 'Computer technology is to the information age what mechanization was to the industrial age' (Naisbitt, 1984: 28). When Manuel Castells was asked what is new with the age he calls the Information Age, he quite bluntly responded: 'It's information technology, that's what is new. The kind of information and communication technologies we have today makes possible that the core of the economy of the whole planet works as a unit'.[2]

Case vignette 3.1: Call centres and globalization

One of the most vivid examples that show how technological infrastructures (in this case, international telephone connections) enable globalization is the move of many telephone enquiries (such as personnel services of large companies), telemarketing and telesales activities to India.[3] For example, the Indian company ExlService,[4] located in Noida (near New Delhi), provides back office processes, contact centre operations and web-based customer care to global corporations. One of the services it provides for American mortgagers is contacting defaulters. In order to be able to contact the American target population of debtors, the Indian employees have to work during the night. They try to persuade or force the defaulters to pay, using the relative anonymity of intercontinental telephone networks. If anybody asks where the employees of the call centre are calling from, they are trained to say that they are calling from Atlanta.[5]

This situation is used here to illustrate at least two key features of the Information Society. First, we witness what is called in the literature 'the death of distance'. Network technology enables workers in India to keep pace with the different time zones in the United States, rendering time and distance less relevant. Indeed, it seems like the world has shrunk because of the availability of information and communication technologies.

Second, we witness how technology is intrinsically linked to the notion of 'culture' and 'identity'. The call centre operators apparently morph their identities using the anonymity of technological networks, disguising the fact that they are actually in India. In other occasions, we see how minorities deliberately use technology to pronounce their original culture.

Economic developments

Second, and another angle on explaining the rise of the Information Society, is the growth of economic activity that is directly connected to informational activities, such as education, law, publishing, media and software engineering (Machlup, 1962; Porat, 1977a, 1977b). Porat distinguished primary and secondary information sectors: the primary sector refers to companies producing intangible information products, and the secondary sector refers to informational activities (such as research and development) within corporations and public administration. Together, according to Porat, they account for almost half of the United States' gross national product (GNP) (Webster, 2002).

Occupational developments

Third, and especially favoured by sociologists (Webster, 2002), is the decline of actual work being done in the manufacturing industry, and the rise of employment in the services sector. In other words, blue collar work is increasingly being replaced by white collar work. Webster concluded that '[s]ince the raw material of non-manual labour is information ... then substantial increase in such informational work can be said to announce the arrival of an information society' (Webster, 2002: 14). About 70 per cent of employment is now found in the white collar service sector of our contemporary societies (in Western Europe, Japan, and North America). In this specific economic sector, wealth production does not come from actually carrying out manual labour, but from decomposing, recombining and applying ideas, knowledge, skills, talent and creativity (Florida, 2004; Leadbeater, 1999). Many commentators have suggested that today's most influential people are knowledge workers, who have the skills and talent to basically manipulate information. Gouldner (1979) even refers to this group of people as a 'new class' of professionals and technical intelligentsia, who are less prone to be subject to either traditional or rationalized authority in organizations.

Case vignette 3.2: (De)skilling and the demise of blue collar work

Occupational developments highlight both qualitative and quantitative changes in ways in which tasks are actually carried out. An example of these changes is the change in job requirements for staff responsible for receiving and distributing postal mail in large organizations (post and mail room services). Only a few decades ago, mail rooms were populated by staff with relatively low levels of literacy. The logistics of letters and parcels required basic understanding of procedures, and the ability to decipher written addresses or locations. Since a couple of years, however, computers have entered post and mail rooms, for the purpose of registering and keeping track of parcels and mail. This requires that clerks at least have a basic understanding of ICTs and possess higher levels of computer literacy. Although many operations merely require tagging and scanning of barcodes, the overall process is much more complex than before and it requires higher levels of cognitive skills. What used to be a manual labour task (taking in and dispersing goods) was converted into an information process, demanding other kinds of skills of clerks.

Another example is the way operators in chemical plants carry out tasks. Traditionally, operators would inspect and observe chemical or physical processes. Since the introduction of automated computer equipment, with which processes are monitored and measured, their main task centres around sitting behind huge information boards or sets of CRT or TFT monitors. The task of physically monitoring actual processes has been transformed into a task involving monitoring information on displays.

Spatial developments

Fourth, the emergence of telecommunication technology has changed the meaning of 'space' and 'geographic proximity'. ICTs, for example in the form of Wide Area Networks like the Internet, may link different locations within and between offices, towns and regions all over the world. Increasingly, we are all connected to these kinds of networks, which enables us to stay in contact with peers, friends, family and colleagues, wherever we are. Irrespective of whether a university lecturer stays in his office or attends a conference at the other end of the world, he or she can still contact students or correspond with editors. Because of telecommunication technology, the world increasingly becomes a wired (or, increasingly even a wireless yet connected) world. The consequence is that there is a new emphasis on *flows of information* that lead us to revise notions of space and time. Space and time are still relevant, one could say these concepts have not disappeared, but they have become less continuous. Physical or temporal proximity is no longer a necessary condition for contact, coordinative efforts, or transfer of immaterial services. And economic production is less bound to geographical location. Knowledge workers increasingly tend to work wherever they like, whenever they choose to work, and even for whoever they choose to work.

Cultural developments

A fifth and final development is the increase of information that circulates in our societies. Mass media, Internet, cell phones, wireless personal digital assistants (PDA), electronic information walls in the streets which display advertisements and news, these all account for a huge density of available information surrounding and penetrating our personal and professional lives. It has been described as 'media-laden society'. Webster (2002: 20)asserts that 'contemporary culture is manifestly more heavily information laden than any of its predecessors. We exist in a media-saturated environment which means that life is quintessentially about symbolization, about exchanging and receiving ... messages about ourselves and others'. The Information Society is also a society that is almost literally drenched with information and pervades us with powerful images. According to Poster (1990), this leads humans to haphazardly take what they like from what they encounter, and mix different images without attaching meaning to them. Information Society's culture, so to speak, is fluid and meaningless. These characteristics of the Information Society, however, also enable individuals to construct and shape their identities (Castells calls these 'project identities') (see also case vignette 3.1).

Synthesis: a view of the Information Society

Five related developments have been identified above; taken together they account for a qualitative change in our society. They mark a shift from an industrial society to a post-industrial society (Bell, 1973). Economic production no longer thrives upon physical labour and products, but on manipulating information by white collar knowledge workers who create value out of applying their skills and creativity to information. As Bell said: 'What counts is not raw muscle power, or energy, but information' (Bell, 1973: 127). And what counts for workers is (intellectual) skills, unique talents, that they can apply to raw informational materials using ICT tools that enable them to work wherever they like (or are told to do so) whenever they wish (or are told to do so). There is a distinct role for technology in the Information Society in the sense that it either drives or enables the trend towards an informational mode of production that is immaterial. It is not bound to geographic location (production can be achieved anywhere, any place and is therefore globalized) and much more flexible than the means for growth used in the previous, industrial society.

An example in which the above-mentioned developments coincide is the development of software. Software development is a knowledge-intensive process. It requires highly skilled workers who use information and communication technology (development tools, modelling tools, and so forth) to transform ideas, concepts, in short, knowledge, by applying systematic knowledge and creativity, into code (that is, programmes). A notable development is that the production of software in large software houses is not geographically concentrated in one office or in one location. Typically, it takes place all over the world, by programmers working in India, Europe, the United States and South-East Asian countries. In each of these countries, skilled knowledge workers code programmes, and by the end of the day their results are transferred electronically (using telecommunication networks) to co-workers in other time zones where production is continued. Consequently, the informational mode of production is being done at a specific geographic location, but the process as a whole is less bound by geographic or temporal restrictions. It is globalized.

Paradoxes and challenges of the Information Society

Introduction

With the developments sketched in the previous section, I described the contours of the Information Society and the characteristics that differentiate the Information Society from the Industrial Society. The concept of Information Society is, however, yet to be analysed in terms of the problems it presents, the issues it has raised, and what the possible consequences are. In this section, I will identify these issues and translate them into paradoxes and challenges for the Information Society. I will do this by following an important contemporary author in the field, the Spanish urban sociologist and ethnographer Manuel Castells. Castells is arguably one of the better known observers and commentators of the Information Society. He may not be the most original scholar in the field, but his work echoes many policy proposals and policy programmes that have been written throughout the world. This is the reason I have explicitly chosen to use his work for exploring the Information Society.[6]

Castells: Information Societies as informational capitalism

Manuel Castells was born in 1942 and lived in Madrid, Cartagena, Valencia and Barcelona. He studied Law and Economics at the University of Barcelona, and became interested in neo-Marxist theories. During the reign of Spanish dictator Franco, Castells had to leave Spain and moved to France, where he studied at the Sorbonne (completion of Master's in 1964) and University of Paris (PhD in 1967).

Castells lectured in sociology and urban studies, and was appointed Professor in Sociology and Urban Planning at the University of California. He nowadays travels around the world, frequently visiting Barcelona and Berkeley.

In his work he has developed a number of research themes in various periods. Roughly from 1967 until 1983, Castells analysed the city as structure (*système urbaine*) with inherent conflicts between various societal groups. His main thesis in this period of time is that the spatial manifestation of cities results from the struggle between these groups (in dialectic, neo-Marxist terms the ruling class and the class that is being dominated by the ruling class). In this struggle, there is, according to the 'early' Castells, a limited role for government: the role for government is dependent on the question who the ruling class is in a specific time frame.

Between 1983 and 1996, Castells seemed to be struck by the observation that because of the emergence of new information and communication technology, the notion of 'place' is less relevant than before, yet the struggle between ruling class and classes that are being ruled does not cease to exist. Based on these observations, Castells established his fame in the field of studies of the Information Society with his trilogy of 1200 pages entitled *The Information Age*. This trilogy is sometimes cited as being the most encyclopedic and developed analysis of the role of information in the present period (Webster, 2002). Characteristic for the approach set out in the three volumes is the empirical orientation: Castells not only theorizes about the Information Society at a conceptual level, but also uses vast amounts of empirical data (most of the times in the form of references to OECD and UN official statistics) as backing for his claims.

Being a former Marxist,[7] Castells emphasizes 'mode of production', the role of capital in globalization ('hypercapitalism'), and matters of inclusion and exclusion of social classes.

Central to Castells' argument about the emergence of the Information Society has been the interpretation of the Industrial Age as embracing a mode of production governed by a so-called 'space of places'. This concept implies that the production of material goods was necessarily concentrated in specific geographic locations, depending on the need for and availability of labour and capital in those locations. According to Castells' line of reasoning, the emergence of telecommunication networks has rendered the 'space of places' less relevant. The 'space of places' is in the Information Society replaced by a new form of spatial logic, which he refers to as 'space of flows'. The space of flows refers to information flowing to and from capital markets, information services being exchanged from supplier to buyers, logistic information, and so on. The space of flows not only enables the functioning of a global marketplace (it is not relevant where production of especially immaterial services takes place, as long as the outputs can be transferred to the customer, anywhere in the world), but also represents the processes that determine the economic, social and symbolic lives of all people. It can be said that information networks have, through the creation of spaces of flow, given rise to informational capitalism. This includes information, and with it capital, flowing freely to wherever its profitability is optimal, in a very flexible way and in real time.

An example of a 'space of flow' is the transfer of transactions on stock markets throughout the world. Transactions across stock markets in Tokyo, Frankfurt, Paris, London, New York, and so forth, occur using telecommunication networks that connect these stock markets. Because of the availability of these networks, geographic proximity of markets has become less relevant, and capital flows in real time from one place to another. One could say that with these information flows, it is not only transactions that are accomplished, but also economic power that is transferred over spaces of flow.

With the concept of spaces of flow, geographical location is not rendered completely irrelevant. Various geographic locations, that are of interest with respect to the space of flows (because talented people with the right skill set are living there, or because they accommodate necessary resources), are integrated into the 'network society'. The Information Society, according to Castells, thus displays geographic discontinuity in the sense that networks connect relevant locations or regions that are not necessarily adjacent or otherwise mutually related. In his line of reasoning, spaces of flow are connected to physical location in at least three ways (Lips, 2005):

- by the technological infrastructure (if a stock market is not connected to a telecommunications network, it cannot be reached by the space of flows);
- by the location of the hubs in the network (in the above example, the stock markets function as a node in a global business network, but the topology of the electronic network does not necessarily have to overlap with the physical topology);
- by the physical presence of the elite that governs the world economy, in terms of their whereabouts and places where they prefer to stay and communicate with each other (top class hotels, VIP rooms in airports).

Castells argues that increasingly our society is organized by means of space of flows at the expense of space of places. That is why it can be called an Information Society. In an Information Society, capital flows quickly (in 'time-less time') from one location to another, thus enabling ultimately flexible modes of production in what Castells calls 'network enterprises'. Telecommunication networks are central to the Information Economy, and knowledge workers increasingly populate the labour market rendering manual labour less relevant.

In the Information Society, it is flexibility that counts. This is probably why Castells favours the concept of the networked enterprise over a traditional view of a large, vertically integrated trans-national corporation. Castells asserts that trans-national corporations are moving from being vertically integrated to being so disintegrated as to transform into a horizontal corporation. This is a corporation in which knowledge workers operate through networks, fixing deals here and there, working on a project that finds a market niche, and thereby owing more commitment to people like themselves, than to the particular company which, for the time being, happens to employ them. Castells suggests that the days of hierarchical control in large trans-national organizations are over and that the core of organizations is an organizational network of 'self-programmed, self-directed units based on decentralization, participation and co-ordination' (Castells, 1996: 166).

Castells' picture of the Information Society presents a number of paradoxical concepts, which have consequences for the fabric of the Information Society itself. As I will show later on, they also have consequences for the role and function of government in the Information Society.

Paradox 1: glocalization

The first paradox is the irrelevance of the localization of modes of production since capital flows swiftly over information networks to wherever it is most profitable, resulting in globalization. As opposed to the centrality of knowledge workers who possess specific skill sets and make deliberate choices as to where to live and where to work, depending on climate, culture, recreational facilities and so on. All that matters to knowledge workers is the degree to which they are connected to the telecommunication networks that keep them 'wired' to employers, peers, colleagues and clients. Castells therefore foresees the emergence of the informational city, 'an urban system with sociospatial structure and dynamics determined by a reliance of wealth, power, and culture, on knowledge and information processing in global networks, managed and organized through intensive use of ICTs' (Castells, 1999: 27). Economic modes of production become, at the same time, globalized in spaces of flow, as well as localized in various (mutually connected) informational cities.

Paradox 2: the Net and the Self

The second paradox Castells himself notices is the antithetic relationship between the spaces of flow as representation of economic and political power (the 'Net'), and the new forms of identities that people are creating in order to defend themselves against the overwhelming power of the Net. Castells describes how people using telecommunication technologies such as the Internet attempt to create identities and to connect with like-minded individuals. He uses the Zapatista movement in Mexico as an example of how a movement can use Internet technology to create and morph identity and meaning. Note that these countermovements cannot be seen as simple reactions to the stress and strains of the Information Society, since representatives of the countermovement to the Net employ information and communication technologies. They use the Information Society to aid their organization and to disseminate their points of view.

Paradox 3: the demise of the working class and the rise of information workers

Furthermore Castells asserts that in the Information Society, there is a new antithetic relationship between classes. In the Industrial Society, the primary antithetic relationship was between the working class and representatives of capital, the entrepreneurs. However, in the Information Society, this has changed dramatically.

First, manual labour is increasingly being automated or otherwise being marginalized. As has been shown previously, in the Information Society, the larger part of the labour market is occupied by information workers.

Second, while the working class traditionally might have been subordinate to the owners of capital, it was widely accepted that it was also indispensable to the entrepreneurial class. Nowadays, a new class emerges – informational labour – which makes the 'old class' disposable.

> Informational labour acts on generic labour in ways which make abundantly clear who is most important to society. It does this in diverse ways, such as by automating generic work out of existence ... or by transferring production to other parts of the world ... or by creating a new product towards which generic labour, being fixed and rigid, is incapable of adjusting.
>
> (Webster, 2002: 112)

Furthermore, there is the rise of a new class of unskilled labour force which simply is irrelevant to informational capitalism because they lack resources of capital and skills. Castells refers to this class as the 'fourth world'. As opposed to the new ruling class of information workers, they do not have the skills to train and retrain in necessary skills themselves.

State and Information Society

Many authors have identified a diminished role for the nation state or national government in the Information Society. Informational capitalism, the mode of informational production and information workers, are less bounded by location and thus by administrative jurisdiction. 'Thus, contemporary information networks of capital, production, trade, science, communication, human rights and crime, bypass the nation state, which, by and large, has stopped being a sovereign entity' (Castells, 2000: 19). One could indeed ask what the role is of a nation state and of a national government that is bound by geographic location, territory and administrative jurisdiction, while the mode of production is not. Knowledge workers have only limited commitments and loyalty to both employers and location, since employment can swiftly be moved from one location to the other. Indeed, traditional models of solidarity and redistribution of wealth, income, and power, become less relevant because the major producers of wealth – information workers – have the utmost flexibility. Their counterparts, however – the unskilled – are still localized and remain a burden on the state's capacity to organize and implement, among other things, social security schemes.

Despite the diminished possibilities for nation states to play a role in the Information Society, however, one could argue that there still is a need for a government to address collective problems of the Information Society.

First, there is still paradoxically a role for governments to play with respect to spatial planning, albeit it is a different role than the traditional role of spatial planning. According to Castells, economic activity flourishes in nodes of the Information Society which he calls *milieux of innovation*. They include for example areas surrounding public universities such as Cambridge (UK), Cambridge (Massachusetts), Stanford (California) and Kyoto (Japan). The planning and governance of these kinds of *science cities* still requires some sort of collective action, moderated by nation states.

Second, a basic requirement of knowledge workers is that they possess the skills, and facilities to train their skills, in order to live up to the requirements of an informational mode of production. Education at all kinds of levels remains an especially important public task in the Information Society.

It remains to be seen whether our current conception of national government and the nation state is still adequate to deal with the challenges of the Information Society. Although Castells contends that there is still a role for the nation state, he also identifies two quite opposing tendencies that will affect its role and position.

The first one is that nation states increasingly operate in supranational networks with other states, such as the European Union, NATO, OECD and GATT. This is to prevent being drawn away in a global maelstrom of information flows. In a sense, nation states display the same type of up scaling as the mode of production more generally in the Information Society.

Second, and arguably more interestingly, the role of local governments is reappraised and they become more significant. Local governments are, in the view of Castells, better suited to deal with the challenges of the Information Society because

- local governments are more representative and thus more legitimized to cater for local, territorialized interests and intensive locally based identities in the Information Society
- local governments are more flexible and thus better able to adapt to ever changing spaces of flow and technological networks (Borja and Castells, 1997).

These issues indicate that the nation state increasingly becomes part of networks: either as part of supranational networks, or in a role as representative of a conglomerate of various local governments.

Case vignette 3.3: Fighting footloose crime

More or less traditional crime fighting is an activity that is bound by jurisdiction of police authorities. With the development of information networks, it has come to the fore that criminal activities, such as money laundering, financial fraud, skimming of bank accounts, and so forth, increasingly take place on information networks, instead of at specific concentrated geographic locations.

Fighting these kinds of criminal activities nowadays takes place under the heading of 'nodal policing'. Nodal policing assumes that digital criminal activity is concentrated at specific 'nodes' of networks, or at places where information networks and physical networks meet, such as airports and sea ports. Nodal policing entails monitoring of activities at these kinds of 'hubs' in physical or informational networks. In order to do so, various authorities with various jurisdictions have to work together. The focus of their activity in monitoring activities and investigating criminal behaviour is not so much the intersected jurisdictions of various authorities (like custom services, national and local police organizations, specialized crime fighting units), but rather the flows of information, people and money. It is hoped that by monitoring these flows of information, preferably at specific hubs where flows meet, it is possible for cooperating agencies to fight fraud and prosecute 'footloose' criminal activity.

Conclusions and discussion

In this chapter, the contours of the Information Society (mainly according to theoreticians such as Bell and Castells) have been portrayed. It has been shown that the impact of technological, social and economic change associated with information and communication technologies stretches beyond the realm of public administration. Rather, an 'Information Society' is emerging that questions the traditional role of the nation state and national governments. This Information State has its own spatial logic, and, more importantly, has a different kind of social structure that raises different challenges and dilemmas.

In this chapter, I have narrowed down theories on the Information Society to lines of reasoning of one of the most influential authors on the Information Society, Manuel Castells. Castells' line of reasoning is heavily influenced by neo-Marxist influences like dialectic terms of In and Out, the Net and the Self, and so on. In the context of the SST line of reasoning in Chapter 1, it is hard to position Castells. On the one hand, Castells himself takes distance from technological determinism. On the other hand, there seems to be an autonomous role for what Castells calls 'network logic'. Moreover, nowhere in Castells' voluminous work is there attention to questions of how technology is being developed, and how technology is shaped in either the design or the implementation stages. Technology seems to appear from 'out there'. As such, Castells uses technological determinism in his line of reasoning.

Over all, commentators, observers and critics of the Information Society have not yet produced a clear image of what is waiting for us to explore. Rather, various trajectories emerge. In the mean time, the role and position of government and public administration is still changing, and so are the technological potentials and information networks.

Discussion questions

1   In many discussions among commentators, academics, politicians, and so forth, the question is being asked what actually is new in the Information Society, and whether there actually are significant differences between the Industrial Age and the Information Age. Do you, in your daily practice, observe events or trends that are associated with the idea of an Information Society?

2   What elements of 'technological determinism' (see Chapter 1) are present in Manuel Castells' line of reasoning?

3   Why does the idea of an Information Society pose challenges to national governments, and why does Castells think that regional and local governments have a prominent role in the Information Society?

4   To what degree do you think that notions of 'space' and 'time' have disappeared in the Information Society? To what degree are they still valid?

5   In the Industrial Age, one of the more important divides in society was the divide between 'capital' and 'labour' (represented by capitalists and workers, respectively). What do you think is the most important divide in the Information Society, and what categories of people can be discerned?

Notes

1 Castells contrasts the Information Society with the Industrial Age, which was, according to Castells, primarily organized around the production and distribution of energy.
2 See http://www.vpro.nl/attachment.db/Interview_Castells.html?17292558 (last visited 10 September 2007).
3 See, for example, http://news.bbc.co.uk/2/hi/south_asia/982023.stm (last visited 10 September 2007).
4 Website http://www.exlservice.com/ (last visited 10 September 2007).
5 See (Dutch) video documentary 'The New World', available for downloading from http://www.vpro.nl/programma/dnw/afleveringen/4217316/ (last visited 10 September 2007).
6 I must apologize that this section probably misrepresents the true spirit of Castells' work, which spans over hundreds of pages. For the sake of brevity I have had to summarize, rephrase and possibly reduce his works considerably.
7 Webster (2002) classified him as a committed social democrat with a passion for politics.

References

Bell, D. (1973). *The Coming of Post-industrial Society*. New York: Basic Books.

Borja, J., and Castells, M. (1997). *Local and Global: Management of Cities in the Information Age*. London: Earthscan.

Castells, M. (1996). *The Rise of the Network Society*. Malden, MA: Blackwell.

Castells, M. (1999). The informational city is a dual city: Can it be reversed? In D. A. Schön, B. Sanyal and W. J. Mitchell (eds) *High Technology and Low-Income Communities: Prospects for the Positive Use of Advanced Information Technology*. Cambridge, MA: MIT Press.

Castells, M. (2000). Materials for an exploratory theory of the network society. *British Journal of Sociology, 51*(1), 5–24.

Florida, R. (2004). *The Rise of the Creative Class*. New York: Basic Books.

Gouldner, A. (1979). *The Future of Intellectuals and the Rise of the New Class* (Vol. 6). London: Macmillan.

Janssen, D., and Rotthier, S. (2005). Trends and consolidations in e-government implementation. In V. J. J. M. Bekkers and V. M. F. Homburg (eds) *The Information Ecology of E-Government: E-Government as Institutional and Technological Innovation*. Amsterdam: IOS Press.

Leadbeater, C. (1999). *Living on Thin Air: The New Economy*. London: Penguin.

Lips, A. M. B. (2005). ICT en samenleving: beelden van de informatiesamenleving. In A. M. B. Lips, V. J. J. M. Bekkers and A. Zuurmond (eds) *ICT en openbaar bestuur: Implicaties en uitdagingen van technologische toepassingen voor de overheid*. Utrecht: Lemma.

Machlup, F. (1962). *The Production and Distribution of Knowledge in the United States*. Princeton, NJ: Princeton University Press.

Naisbitt, J. (1984). *Megatrends: Ten New Directions Transforming our Lives*. New York: Futura.

Porat, M. U. (1977a). *The Information Economy: Sources and Methods for Measuring the Primary Information Sector (Detailed Industry Records)*. Washington, DC: US Department of Commerce, Office of Telecommunications.

Porat, M. U. (1977b). *The Information Economy: Sources and Methods for Measuring the Primary Information Sector (Detailed Industry Records)*. Washington, DC: US Department of Commerce, Office of Telecommunications.

Poster, M. (1990). *The Mode of Information: Poststructuralism and Social Context*. Cambridge: Polity.

Webster, F. (2002). *Theories of the Information Society*. London: Routledge.

4 Bureaucracy and virtual organizations

Key points

After reading this chapter, you will be able to

- define 'bureaucracy' and explain the underlying characteristics of the Weberian ideal type of bureaucracy
- explain why technology has rendered some of the raisons d'être of the ideal type of bureaucracy less relevant
- explain what is meant by virtual or post-bureaucratic organizations
- explain what difficulties are posed by post-bureaucratic organizations in the public sector.

Introduction

In Chapter 3, I reflected on the relation between information and communication technologies and the macro level. It has been shown that the relevance of ICTs stretches beyond changes in public administration, and leads to a reappraisal and repositioning of the idea of government. Having said this, this does not imply that ICTs do not have ramifications for public administration itself. In this chapter, I therefore focus on the relation between 'smart machines', as I have called ICTs in Chapter 2, and the idea of 'bureaucracy'. Since the beginning of the twentieth century, the ideal type of bureaucracy has had a strong influence upon the organization of public administration. This has occurred both in a rhetorical, normative sense, as well as in the practice of administrative and political life.

Bureaucracy is, on the one hand, required for reasons of impartiality and neutrality and because of its ability to impersonally apply rational rules over specific jurisdictions (Behn, 2001). Behn (2001) refers to this connotation of bureaucracy as the 'classic' public administration paradigm.

On the other hand, bureaucracy, especially in the second half of the twentieth century and at the beginning of the twenty-first century, is a bad word (Nohria and Berkley, 1994). It is associated with cumbersome operations, lack of efficiency, dysfunctional compartmentalization and hence, diminished responsiveness (Duivenboden and Lips, 2005). Many politicians, organization theorists and practitioners have, as a result, attempted to reform bureaucracy, reduce red tape, 'bust' bureaucracy, create entrepreneurial government and so on (Homburg and Bekkers, 2005). Many reforms are inspired by the wish to overcome the cumbersome associated with bureaucracies, and especially public bureaucracies. Organization theorists like Daniel Bell (1973), Shoshana Zuboff (1988), William Davidow and Thomas Malone (1992), as well as public administration scholars like Arre Zuurmond (1994) and Victor Bekkers (1998a, 1998b, 2001), have reflected upon new organizational forms. They identify the potential for using smart machines to relax some of the distressing principles of bureaucracy, while at the same time attempting to maintain its virtues. They adopt the admittedly voguish terms 'post-bureaucratic organization' and 'virtual organization' to describe the possibilities they foresee. In these new organizational forms, the coordination of work in and between organizations is no longer achieved primarily through hierarchies, but rather mediated through information and communication technologies. In virtual organizations, there is supposed to be a less tangible hierarchical structure, and organizational boundaries are less fixed and more permeable, making intra-organizational and inter-organizational cooperation less strenuous. Furthermore, because ICTs enable telecommuting, an ICT-enabled organization is not necessarily concentrated on a specific geographic location. The organization can be anywhere, because information and communication technologies enable its members to coordinate efforts and exchange information without necessarily being concentrated in a physical location. To this extent, the word virtual in virtual organizations refers to the power of information and communication technology to reconfigure organizations. Underlying processes and social interactions change dramatically, making more or less traditional conceptions of organizations as rationalized, physical entities less inevitable. This is in stark contrast to the organizations once sought by theorists like Fayol, Taylor, Gulick, Urwick and Weber.

Case vignette 4.1: Virtual libraries (part 1)

An example of virtual organizations is provided by the world of libraries. Both public as well as university libraries have, already for a couple of decades, transformed themselves from physical book warehouses to information factories. This has occurred in at least two senses.

First, many books and papers have been made available digitally and can be accessed anywhere, any place. The physical manifestation of books and reports in some cases still exist, but in many other cases the physical embodiment of paper files has simply disappeared and moved to digital repositories. In this sense, the library organization is a virtual organization. It is based on immaterial assets and is separate from the localization of staff, thus virtual in nature.

Second, as far as actual physical books, journals and other paper resources are concerned, libraries throughout the world have implemented automated cataloguing systems. These make it possible to search remote catalogues and request copies of books that are available only at another library's premises. To an ordinary library user, these kinds of cataloguing systems render existing organizational boundaries less relevant. It no longer matters where a specific book is located, as long as it can be swiftly transferred to a location where it can be picked up.

In this chapter, the concept of virtual organization is explored by, among other things, focusing upon the role of smart machines in making bureaucracy work. First, the ideal type of bureaucracy is depicted and foundations of bureaucracy are explored, including its technology and conception of information. Second the characteristics of modern ICTs that question the foundations and raison d'être of bureaucracy as an ideal type are described and discussed. Third, several types and examples of virtual organizations in public administration are discussed, and finally conclusions and further questions are presented.

Conceptual foundations of bureaucracy

Origins of bureaucracy

Before jumping into an analysis of this voguish idea of virtual, boundary-less, flat organizational forms, the origins of bureaucracy need to be explored. After all, 'bureaucracy' is used to denote typical organizational forms in public administration. In general, the bureaucratic organization has its roots, first, in scientific management as pioneered and advocated by, among others, Henri Fayol and Frederick Taylor, and second, in Weber's theory of bureaucratization.

Fayol and Taylor as inspirators of industrial bureaucracy

Henri Fayol and Frederick Taylor pioneered the field of organization theory at the end of the nineteenth and beginning of the twentieth centuries. They suggested and implemented principles of scientific management and classical management theory.[1] Their contributions to the discipline of organization theory should be interpreted in the context of scientific and technological developments. Mechanization, engineering and natural sciences gained prominence and resulted in various technological innovations that were applied in industries. Both Fayol and Taylor were engineering-oriented executive managers with hands-on managerial experiences, by no means purely academic organization theorists. They both observed in the organizations they managed (the French mining industry in the case of Fayol, and the US steel industry in the case of Frederick Taylor) that the way in which tasks were carried out, suffered from lack of planning and control. This had negative consequences for workers who had to toil, for bosses who were unable to adequately direct processes of work, and for efficiency in general.

Henri Fayol (1841–1925) was a mining engineer who was struck by the importance of management as a separate organizational activity. Although Fayol viewed organizations as essentially social phenomena, he preferred to apply principles from the (natural) sciences and engineering to processes of management. From this perspective management should be based on systematically gathered observations, and Fayol strived to discover universal 'laws' of organizing. Transparent hierarchies with clear line of authority and accountability, and especially clear lines of communication between functionally differentiated units and management was Fayol's contribution to management.

From Taylor's perspective, the type of large organizations he was familiar with, suffered from slack, inefficiency and toiling by workers and could be improved and rationalized. In essence he saw that these phenomena could be attributed to the lack of control in organizations. Through time-and-motion studies, Taylor attempted to observe, in a scientifically valid way,[2] slack and toiling in organizations. However, being a practice-oriented, in some ways obsessed engineer, he also attempted to design and implement measures that were meant to fight slack and inefficiency in processes (and thus, to 'rationalize' processes). Overall, Taylor sought measures and principles that, when applied, resulted in a universal, best way of organizing. These measures included the following:

- Decomposition of physical tasks into smaller activities that could easily be standardized, trained and measured (*horizontal* decomposition of tasks).
- The selection and training of workers to fit the task they were allocated to.
- Separation of physical labour ('the hand') from more or less mental or intellectual labour ('the brain': management and engineering) (*vertical* decomposition of tasks). So, managers should do what they were supposed to be good at (thinking), and workers were to be assigned to the activities they were supposed to be good at (implementation).
- Concentrating development and improvement activities in separate organizational units, for the sake of better controlling tasks and processes.

Central to the idea of organizing in Taylor's view seems to be the concept of *control*. Control, achieved through horizontal and vertical decomposition of tasks, standardization and monitoring, and in general clear separation of tasks and responsibilities, is supposed to result in more efficient operations in organizations. Separation of tasks enabled specialization and training (and organizations could also be manned by interchangeable workers and even managers) since tasks that are functionally differentiated are easier to train, monitor and supervise. Control, one might say, appears through decomposing and recombining knowledge. Taylor's goal was to isolate (by means of vertical decomposition) knowledge of the organization from production to create 'management' that could serve as a repository and processor of expropriated knowledge (Webster and Robins, 1986).

Control is also central to Weber's connotation of bureaucracy. As Weber himself noted: 'bureaucratic administration means fundamentally the exercise of control on the basis of knowledge' (Weber, 1947: 339).

Taylor himself was severely criticized for his line of reasoning. By the time of his death in 1915, he was commonly regarded to be the 'enemy' of the working class. Workers and managers in the Bethlehem Steel Company, in which Taylor implemented some of his insights, argued that Taylor's view would result in dehumanizing tendencies (both for workers as well as for managers). In 1911, Taylor was also summoned to appear before a committee of the US House of Representatives. However, the mechanisms of management and organizing he described and prescribed can also be seen as parts of a much broader trend or social force involving the rationalization and, in the nineteenth century, mechanization of life (Morgan, 1986).

Weber as founding father of rationalized organizational design

Max Weber also contributed to our contemporary bureaucracies, albeit from a less operational, mechanistic way of reasoning. He tended to view the bureaucratic form of organization as the inescapable telos of modern society: he assumed that only the bureaucracy is suited to otherwise unmanageable complexity of the modern organization (Groth, 1999). Bureaucracy, according to Weber, is a form of organization that emphasizes precision, speed, clarity, regularity, reliability and efficiency through a fixed division of tasks, hierarchical supervision and detailed rules and regulations. Weber's explanation for the existence of bureaucracy was also influenced by the wish to replace traditional and charismatic forms of authority with what he referred to as rational authority. Rationalized authority by means of clear lines of authority and functional differentiation could eliminate, for example, corruption and fraudulent organizational behaviour. Weber was not the first to note the need to rationalize organizations – Wilson (1887) noted with respect to the American administration at the end of the nineteenth century, 'the poisonous atmosphere of [city] government, the crooked secrets of state administration, the confusion, sinecurism and corruption ever again discovered in the bureaux at Washington' (Wilson, 1887: 206) – but he is the sociologist best known for vigorously studying the social antecedents of organizations in larger societies.

Organizational structure and material files as the backbones

According to the 'classic' public administration paradigm, bureaucracies have to be based on principles of public service in order to prevent corruption (Groth, 1999; Guy Peters, 1996). These principles include:

- an apolitical public service
- hierarchy and rules
- permanence and stability

- use of material files to document rules and regulations as a basis for management
- an institutionalized civil service
- internal regulation
- equality.

They are used to curtail the influence and power of the tiny cogs in the wheels of public sector organizations (Bovens and Zouridis, 2002) and, in general, to map ways that restrict personal, patrimonial and patriarchal modes of governance. In general, we see that the concepts of structure (delineated by authority) and material files are crucial concepts in bureaucracy, at least for two reasons.

First, structure refers to a decomposition of general processes and behaviour for the sake of efficiency, precision and clarity. It is assumed that production can be controlled better if it takes place in neatly described areas of expertise, and that people working within specialized areas of expertise can be trained better to suit their job. They learn more intensively to carry out their (specialized) tasks. In other words, in bureaucracies, departmentalization and decomposition make coordination relatively easy. While rules, regulations and hierarchies reduce chances of unintentional errors, fraud, negligence and opportunistic behaviours by executives, as well as by workers (Tat-Kei Ho, 2002).

Second, and somewhat more advanced in its line of reasoning, structure, conceived of as a set of 'jurisdictional areas' allows for accountability through exposing material files. A core concept in the public administration paradigm is the idea of accountability. This is firmly rooted in the writings of Wilson, Taylor, Weber, Goodnow and Gulick (Behn, 2001) and has been understood as a chain of hierarchical accountability, from citizens to elected officials to appointed officials to government action. A fully developed strict organizational structure allows for information flows directly and exclusively up superiors, administrators and eventually members of parliament. This implies that the concept of structure is, apart from a vehicle for organizational efficiency, a so-called *reification of information requirements*: it enables information flows that are prompted by administrators.

Technology and bureaucracy

According to Nohria and Berkley (1994), smart machines play an explicit role in the ideal typical bureaucracy. They have stated that '[c]omputer systems and software adopted the "architecture" of bureaucracy.... Not surprisingly the language of information systems became the language of bureaucracy' (Nohria and Berkley, 1994: 120). Especially in the early years of digital computer technology (the 'mainframe' era), the principles of bureaucratic organizational design were hard-coded ('enshrined') in technology. In Groth's words:

> the Weber/Taylor bureaucracy is a highly structured input-output system, in which a 'store of documentary material' (Weber's own phrase) is maintained ... one might say that bureaucracy functions as a computer, as an ingenious

way of instantiating the mechanistic, highly functionalized workings of a computer in a physical arrangement of people, paper, and rules.

(Groth, 1999: 118)

In conclusion, one can say that smart machines in bureaucracies embody and reify flows of documentary materials. According to Zuboff's (1988) informating capacities (see Chapter 2), smart machines enable exercising control by allowing superiors to monitor the behaviour of lower-level employees. As such, smart machines are any bureaucrat's instruments for control, reliability and accountability.

Questioning the foundations of bureaucracy

Contender 1: the New Public Management (NPM)

The concept of bureaucracy has been severely criticized since the 1980s for rigidity, proceduralism, inefficiency, incapability to serve human clients with preferences and feelings (Bozeman, 2000), inaccessibility for citizens because of heavy compartmentalization and so on. One manifestation of anti-bureaucracy resentments was the upcoming clamour throughout the Western world for administrative reform (for example, by means of new public management techniques) (Behn, 1998, 2001; Osborne and Gaebler, 1992; Pollitt, 2000; Pollitt and Bouckaert, 2000; Rhodes, 1991). The literature lists a wealth of reforms under the heading of NPM. In general, one finds the following (Pollitt et al., 2007):

- the use of rather lean and highly decentralized structures, like semi-autonomous organizations, rather than large, multipurpose, hierarchical ministries or departments;
- the use of divisional structures in public service resulting in breaking down former unitary bureaucracies, as well as in inter-organizational relations with organizations in private and voluntary sectors, resulting in blurred and broadened frontiers between the public sector, the market sector and the voluntary sector;
- a widespread emphasis on contracts (or contract-like relationships) instead of formal, hierarchical relationships, and a much wider-then-hitherto deployment of markets (or market-type) mechanisms (MTMs) for the delivery of public services;
- more attention on the management of organizations and management skills of public servants – as opposed to policy advice and legal skills which were dominant in the classic public administration paradigm;
- a shift in the focus of management systems and efforts from inputs like staff or buildings, and processes (for example teaching, inspecting) towards outputs (test results, inspection reports) and outcomes (safety, health, standards of literacy in the community)

- a shift towards more measurement and quantification, especially in the form of systems of performance indicators and/or explicit standards.

Core to new public management seems to be the conviction that democracy can only survive by delivering services efficiently (which is an aim in itself), either by adopting a market orientation or by reengineering the public service itself (which are *means* to the *end* of efficient service delivery). In terms of accountability, there is a shift from accountability for process (finances and fairness) to accountability for performance (Behn, 1998, 2001). According to Behn (1998), accountability for process is achieved through record keeping by agencies, which are inspected by (independent or hierarchically superior) auditors for compliance with respect to regulations. If irregularities are observed, individuals are disciplined.

Basically, in new public management, there is an ambition to bypass or complement a hierarchical accountability route which is seen as cumbersome, slow, inefficient and unproductive, by using a system of accountability to 'customers' of government services, using direct mechanisms like user fees, surveys, and user panels much like an enterprise checks whether its goods or services meet customers' requirements.

How these underlying ideas and their implementation take shape in various countries fluctuates enormously (Pollitt et al., 2007). This may be due to characteristics of the specific institutional settings new public management ideas and practices are implemented in (in terms of starting points, path dependencies, implementation competencies) (Hood, 2000), but it may also be attributed to the heterogeneous nature of the concept of new public management itself (Lynn, 1998).

Contender 2: virtual organizations

Administrative reform, for example under the heading of the label of 'new public management', was not the only contender to the classic bureaucracy. In 1992, the anti-bureaucracy campaign was fuelled from a different angle with the publication of the first management book about *virtual organizations*. And whereas NPM was predominantly portrayed as a *managerial revolution*, the rhetoric of virtual organizations also included a technological component of administrative change. In *The Virtual Corporation*, Davidow and Malone (1992) emphasized the revolutionary (as opposed to the consolidating) power of technology with respect to (private, industrial) bureaucracies. They claimed that information and communication technologies did not *necessarily* reify bureaucracy's structure and practices, but moreover questioned the foundations of bureaucracy, giving rise to new organizational forms. At the heart of Davidow and Malone's line of reasoning was the conviction that technology could help to do away with the constraints and limitations that have been inherent in the concept of bureaucracy (Groth, 1999). The then upcoming network technology could, according to Davidow and Malone (1992), contest the basic foundations of bureaucracy because of the following characteristics (Groth, 1999):

- Weber's material files, that guided behaviour in bureaucracy, could reappear in a much less tangible, yet more pervasive form, namely as flexible and electronic scripts that either replace or sublimely guide human activities (see also Zuboff's informating capacities, Chapter 2).
- Face-to-face communication and coordination could be complemented with, or sometimes even replaced by, computer-mediated communication as a means of conducting primary activities within organizations.
- The idea of organizational structure as a medium for control could be replaced by the notion of an information infrastructure. Behaviour is no longer guided by means of hierarchical control and fiat, but by means of the information that is presented to employees, or by means of access to information resources an employee has. Paradoxically, for the observer the functioning of an organization appears spontaneous and structureless, yet control in practice is much more pervasive (Zuurmond, 1994).
- The capability of technology to connect individuals from various departments and organizations, and the exchange of information among them, could blur legal boundaries between departments and make them less relevant than in the ideal typical bureaucratic structure.
- The idea of highly specialized tasks could be replaced by cross-functional jobs, enabled by ICTs (notably expert systems and decision-support systems).

Defining virtual organizations

From the emergence of administrative reform, and from the notion of technological reforms of bureaucracy, it is possible to describe and define a new form of organization, the virtual organization. Bellamy and Taylor (1998: 36) define virtual organizations as 'a set of interdependent information mediated processes conducted over the wires across a network of suppliers, distributors and customers'. Characteristic of virtual organizations is that the shopfloor of production does not necessarily have to be concentrated on one physical location, as network technology can also 'wire' and coordinate activities of dislocated individuals or units. Cooperation between individuals or units in a virtual organization can be temporal, and depending upon the desired outcome, required resources are pooled. Whenever the outcome has been achieved, the organization can be dismantled. Bekkers (2001) characterizes virtual organizations as 'work spaces', as opposed to work places, in which humans interact with each other mediated by ICTs. They share information and knowledge in such a way that a different kind of reality is created. Information and communication technology is thus a vital concept in virtual organizations, and because specific implementations of ICTs in virtual organizations render much of the bureaucratic logic irrelevant, the Weberian, public administration paradigm of bureaucracy is implicitly or explicitly overturned. As Groth states, 'we witness the vilification of hierarchy, the physical abolition of the 'office', the disappearance of office rules, the reintegration of the levels of planning and execution, and other such inversions of Weber's ideal type' (Groth, 1999: 116). Therefore, this new, emerging virtual organization is also referred to as a *post-bureaucratic* organization.

Examples of virtual organizations

RINIS: an information intermediary in Dutch social security

An example of a virtual organization in the public sector is RINIS (Homburg, 1999).[3] RINIS is both a very minimal organizational structure (it is a foundation and is staffed by a general manager and a small number of technical support staff specialists) and an information infrastructure that connects various executive institutions in the system of Dutch social security. RINIS's business is to enable exchange of information between various autonomous agencies that execute specific pieces of social insurance legislation, tax agencies, municipal social service agencies and so on. A board consisting of representatives of the various participating organizations governs the RINIS organization. The existence of the RINIS concept enables participating organizations to check clients' information at other institutions. Whereas organizational barriers still exist formally in terms of information exchange, these barriers exist to a lesser extent. Based on mutual agreements, the participants exchange information using the RINIS information infrastructure (so, RINIS delivers primarily data services: see Chapter 5). The information exchange does not take place under specific administrative fiat, other than the collective fiat of the representative organizations, and makes the boundaries of the participating organizations permeable and flexible. A primary objective of the participating organizations is to exchange information for detecting fraud. They do this by exchanging and sharing client information without actually fully referring clients or full client information from one organization to the other.

Virtual organizations in penal law enforcement

Grijpink (1997) describes the VIPS system,[4] an information system for use in the (Dutch) value chain for penal law enforcement. It is a system in which hundreds of public and semi-public authorities and private partners cooperate to ensure security and law enforcement. Examples of organizations that participate in this chain are the District Attorney (in Dutch: 'Openbaar Ministerie'), Court ('rechtbank'), Prison System ('gevangeniswezen'), Probation and After-Care Service ('reclassering'). VIPS enables the organizations to exchange information as if no organizational boundaries exist. In practice, the participating organizations' databases continue to exist, but software components are used to facilitate the communication (and not so much the registration) of data. In order to accomplish this, Grijpink proposes the following 'building blocks':

- referring: an automated catalogue with reference information
- numbering: a historically unique numbering system (name, number or combination of the two) to indicate objects in databases
- verifying: a limited set of queries with the possible results 'Yes' or 'No'.

In this case, it is possible for organizations to control their own database and to ensure appropriate access rights, while enabling other organizations' to access internal information systems in a rather controlled, agreed-upon way. The virtual enforcement organization is based on a number of pillars:

- autonomy of participating organizations by emphasizing communication rather than registration
- focusing on local, decentralized databases
- an emphasis on decentral arrangements about access and availability of data. There are a few agreed-upon central communication building blocks like referring, numbering and verifying functions in networks of organizations.

Overall, one can see that because of the VIPS system, existing organizations are able to exchange information on suspects and convicted criminals and with that, coordinate activities across traditional, bureaucratic organizational boundaries in a rather flexible way. In this way, VIPS embodies a virtual penal law organization. It enables the cooperation between various existing bureaucracies, using other means than classic bureaucratic control through structure and hierarchy.

The ethics of virtual organizations

The vilification of structure?

The examples described in the previous section indicate that smart machines do not necessarily replicate and reify bureaucratic structures. Rather, smart machines can be put to use to achieve control and coordination by means other than traditional bureaucratic techniques such as strict hierarchy and control through formalization and material files. Bureaucratic control thus makes way for the 'virtual control' that is *enshrined* in smart machines. The daily work routine of street-level bureaucrats that execute legislation in the field of social security (see RINIS example), librarians (PICA example in case vignette 4.2), magistrates, law enforcers and social workers (see VIPS) becomes increasingly determined by information that is provided to them through information infrastructures of smart machines, rather than by direct control by superiors. Knowledge workers in today's knowledge-intensive organizations are almost completely dependent upon access to smart machines (email facilities, PDAs, and so on), with their activities being often fully determined by information that is provided to them through smart machines. Zuurmond (1994) has coined the term 'infocracy' to denote types of organizations in which control is not sought through hierarchy and rules, but rather through *informational control*.

The emergence of virtual control in public administration is, however, not without problems. Several practical but also normative sets of questions arise.

Case vignette 4.2: Virtual libraries (part 2)

The case of virtual libraries (see case vignette 4.1) provides an example of how virtual organizations display organizational stress and political manoeuvring (Wierda, 1991). In the Netherlands, in order to enable library users to browse catalogues of all university libraries, PICA was set up. PICA (an acronym for *Project for Integrated Catalogue Information*) is a joint project of the Dutch libraries, initiated by the Dutch Minister of Education and Sciences, and executed by a separate organization, the Cooperative Body Royal Library and University Library PICA, founded in 1969. It should be noted that the development of PICA was rather problematic, labour intensive and prone to political manoeuvring. During the development, all participants had second thoughts:

> [A]ll respondents feared losing part of their independence, which was a major cause for several libraries to be cautious, or even hostile, towards the effort to develop (the system ...). [D]ifferences of opinion with respect to communication protocols and with respect to description formats were major points in which the mutual conflicts were expressed.
>
> (Wierda, 1991: 54–55)

This resulted in a lack of commitment by participants and even manifest opposition towards the rather centralized structure of the new joint system. However, eventually, the system was effectively put into practice, but not before severe coercion was used by the minister himself.

Public service values

Most of the times, discussions about 'debunking bureaucracy' centre around functional questions, like whether reforms have resulted in a more effective, efficient and responsive government apparatus. However, in the academic discipline of public administration, there exists a longstanding tradition of reflecting on values. Values can be defined as a belief that a specific kind of behaviour or conduct is preferable over alternative conduct. In the ideal type of bureaucracy, there are a number of values, such as impartiality, integrity, rule of law, equality before the law, the emphasis on rational authority, and so forth.

A first set of questions arises because the idea of structure not only serves the purpose of 'control' and guiding behaviour in bureaucratic organizations, but also serves as a chain for vertical accountability, enabling lower-level staff members to report to their superiors and administrators, who report to politicians and others. In strict hierarchies, therefore, there exists means that enable accountability through neatly organized, vertically oriented channels of communication, that are delineated by jurisdictional areas and legally defined organizational boundaries. In the introduction to this chapter, it was explained that hierarchies not only enable control, but also are the reification of accountability requirements prompted by administrators and politicians.

In virtual organizations, through elaborate means of information exchange and interaction, organizational boundaries are blurred and their function to delineate patterns of vertical accountability has ceased to exist. Therefore, the issue of accountability poses serious problems to virtual organizations, since accountability is much harder to organize in structureless, fluid patterns in which work is accomplished. In theory, it is proposed that in virtual, public organizations, the idea of vertical accountability should be replaced or complemented by other forms of accountability, such as *horizontal accountability*. This includes organizations reporting on performance and procedures to peers and citizens rather than to administrators and politicians. In practice, however, this is a rather hard act to follow.

Institutional safeguards

Another 'virtue' of bureaucratic organization, aside from its inherent quality to enable control and serve as a mechanism for promoting vertical accountability, is that it – by design – enables the implementation of safeguards like balances of power and checks and balances. For instance, in the penal law enforcement chain (see VIPS example), duties and responsibilities of magistrates are organizationally separated from tasks and responsibilities of district attorneys. This is for reasons of checks and balances between executive and judicial powers. Unlimited access to and from various branches of power may endanger the separation of powers that is one of the cornerstones of many Western democracies.

Conclusions and discussion

In this chapter, the voguish virtual organization has been introduced. Virtual organizations are relevant for, for example, back office integration. In those kind of initiatives, in order to serve citizens' requests, it is often needed to share information and exchange data on clients without fundamentally restructuring existing organizational structures. The concept of virtual organization makes this possible: it relates to a set of interdependent information-mediated processes conducted over the wires across a network of organizations, units or individual workers, and gives technology (as analysed in Chapter 3) a very specific place. The activities of organizations, units or individuals that comprise the virtual organizations are not guided by formal hierarchy. Instead they are guided by rules, conventions and agreements that are coded in an information infrastructure in which they participate and which they can simultaneously – by means of mutual agreement or any other decision making mechanism – craft, shape and form. In general, one might say that with the emergence of advanced information and communication technologies, organizational structure and hierarchy no longer have to serve as blunt mechanisms for exercising control. Control is now embedded in information infrastructures, in the email facilities and streams of email that structure the daily activities of knowledge workers for example, or in automatic reservation systems that determine the caseload of hospital doctors. Paradoxically, in virtual organizations, control is both strengthened as well as put further behind the scenes. In virtual organizations, traditional filing cabinets of bureaucratic ritual disappear. They are replaced by devices like emailboxes and personal data assistants (PDAs) which have their own built-in schedules to connect and coordinate wirelessly to other people's PDAs.

This does not imply, however, that the relevance of structure does not exist any more. Moreover, bureaucratic control seems to have imploded, withdrawn from everyday experience and the observation of people working in bureaucracies. As has been mentioned in this chapter, ICTs initially replicated bureaucratic structure, but have since made bureaucratic organizations less necessary. This has been fuelled by an anti-bureaucracy resentment, which for example is eminent in new public management techniques, as well as by the growing capabilities of ICTs and their cost-effectiveness. ICTs have lived up to electronic information's ability to overcome the limitations of space and time that had made bureaucratic organizations necessary in the first place.

The empirical question is, however, whether this actually takes place or can take place. As was mentioned in the conclusion of Chapter 3, we may be overly deterministic if we think that technology alone can produce desired effects. Following the social shaping of technology-perspective, it can be expected that the way and degree to which technology is applied interacts with the socio-political context. Therefore, in the next section an empirical analysis is presented of the way information technology can foster information sharing in and between bureaucracies.

Discussion questions

1   More than once, ICTs are being mentioned as instruments for 'bureaucracy bashing'. What characteristics of ICTs (see Chapter 2) make ICTs useful for contesting the idea of bureaucracy?

2   Name and describe occurrences or examples of how ICTs can replace paper-based stores of documentary material. What implications can you think of?

3   Which bureaucratic 'principles' are most contested by specific implementations of ICTs?

4   Explain why ICTs can be used to enhance bureaucratization as well as to debunk and bust bureaucracy.
5   How do you think informational control of public administration can be counterbalanced?

Notes

1   There is a notable difference between the two terms. Scientific management, often associated with the works of Frederick Taylor, is mainly concerned with the rigorous design of tasks and ways in which workers carry out tasks. The focus is thus on the improvement of production methods in specific workshops; scientific management mainly is about the management of production. Classical management theory, on the other hand, is linked to the works of Henri Fayol and focuses on the management of organizations as a whole.
2   With the word 'scientific', Taylor referred to the (natural) sciences.
3   RINIS is the Dutch abbreviation for Routeringsinstituut voor InterNationale InformatieStromen.
4   VIPS is the Dutch acronym for VerwijsIndex Personen Strafrechthandhaving (reference index for penal law enforcement).

References

Behn, R. D. (1998). The New Public Management paradigm and the search for government accountability. *International Public Management Journal, 1*(2), 131–164.

Behn, R. D. (2001). *Rethinking Democratic Accountability*. Washington, DC: Brookings Institution.

Bekkers, V. J. J. M. (1998a). *Grenzeloze overheid. Over informatisering en grensveranderingen in het openbaar bestuur*. Alphen aan den Rijn: Samsom.

Bekkers, V. J. J. M. (1998b). Wiring public organizations and changing organizational juridisctions. In I. T. M. Snellen and W. B. H. J. v. d. Donk (eds) *Public Administration in an Information Age*. Amsterdam: IOS Press.

Bekkers, V. J. J. M. (2001). *Voorbij de virtuele organisatie? Over de bestuurskundige betekenis van virtuele variëteit, contingentie en parallel organiseren*. The Hague: Elsevier Bedrijfsinformatie.

Bell, D. (1973). *The Coming of Post-industrial society*. New York: Basic Books.

Bellamy, C., and Taylor, J. (1998). *Governing in the Information Age*. Buckingham: Open University Press.

Bovens, M., and Zouridis, S. (2002). From street-level bureaucracy to system-level bureaucracy: How information and communication technology is transforming administrative discretion and constitutional control. *Public Administration Review, 62*(2), 174–184.

Bozeman, B. (2000). *Bureaucracy and Red Tape*. Upper Saddle River, NJ: Prentice-Hall.

Davidow, W., and Malone, T. J. (1992). *The Virtual Corporation*. New York: HarperCollins.

Duivenboden, H. P. M. v., and Lips, A. M. B. (2005). Responsive e-government services: Towards 'New' Public Management. In V. J. J. M. Bekkers and V. M. F. Homburg (eds) *The Information Ecology of E-Government: E-Government as Institutional and Technological Innovation in Public Administration*. Amsterdam: IOS Press.

Grijpink, J. H. A. M. (1997). *Keteninformatisering, met toepassing op de justitiële bedrijfsketen* (*Value Chain Information, with Application to the Juridical Supply Chain*). The Hague: SDU.

Groth, L. (1999). Future organizational design. In L. Groth (ed.) *Future Organizational Design*. Chichester: Wiley.

Guy Peters, B. (1996). *The Future of Governing: Four Emerging Models*. Lawrence, KS: University Press of Kansas.

Homburg, V. M. F. (1999). *The Political Economy of Information Management: A Theoretical and Empirical Analysis of Decision Making Regarding Interorganizational Information Systems*. Capelle aan den IJssel: Labyrinth.

Homburg, V. M. F., and Bekkers, V. J. J. M. (2005). E-Government and NPM: A perfect marriage? In V. J. J. M. Bekkers and V. M. F. Homburg (eds) *The Information Ecology of E-Government: E-Government as Institutional and Technological Innovation in Public Adminstration*. Amsterdam: IOS Press.

Hood, C. (2000). Paradoxes of public-sector managerialism, old public management and public service bargains. *International Public Management Journal, 3*(1), 1–22.

Lynn, L. E. (1998). A critical analysis of the New Public Management. *International Public Management Journal, 1*(1), 107–123.

Morgan, G. (1986). *Images of Organization*. Beverley Hills, CA: Sage.

Nohria, N., and Berkley, J. D. (1994). The virtual organization (bureaucracy, technology and the implosion of control). In C. Heckscher and A. Dennelon (eds) *The Post-bureaucratic Organization*. Thousand Oaks, CA: Sage.

Osborne, D., and Gaebler, T. (1992). *Reinventing Government: How the Entrepreneurial Spirit is Transforming the Public Sector*. Reading, MA: Addison-Wesley.

Pollitt, C. P. (2000). Is the emperor in his underwear? An analysis of the impacts of public management reform. *Public Management, 2*(2), 181–199.

Pollitt, C. P., and Bouckaert, G. (2000). *Public Management Reform: A Comparative Analysis*. Oxford: Oxford University Press.

Pollitt, C. P., van Thiel, S., and Homburg, V. M. F. (eds) (2007). *New Public Management in Europe: Adaptation and Alternatives*. Basingstoke: Palgrave Macmillan.

Rhodes, R. (1991). The New Public Management. *Public Administration, 69*(1).

Tat-Kei Ho, A. (2002). Reinventing local governments and the e-government initiative. *Public Administration Review, 62*(4), 434–444.

Weber, M. (1947). *The Theory of Social and Economic Organization*. New York: The Free Press.

Webster, F., and Robins, K. (1986). *Information Technology: A Luddite Analysis*. Norwood, NJ: Ablex.

Wierda, F. W. (1991). *Developing Interorganizational Information Systems*. Delft: Eburon.

Wilson, W. (1887). The study of administration. *Political Science Quarterly, 2*(2), 206.

Zuboff, S. (1988). *In the Age of the Smart Machine: The Future of Work and Power*. New York: Basic Books.

Zuurmond, A. (1994). *De infocratie*. The Hague: Phaedrus.

5 The political economy of information networks

Key points

After reading this chapter, you will be able to

- describe how information exchange can give rise to politicking and political manoeuvring
- analyse information networks in terms of information ownership and incentives to use and update information
- explain how dispersion of control is related to the viability of information networks
- explain how in specific cases information politicking, hoarding of information, and struggle for ownership can be interpreted.

Introduction

It has already been argued that the advent of computing power and information networks brought with it possibility that information can be shared and communicated within, and between, various public bureaucracies. The ideal type of the post-bureaucratic organization is even based on the view that information exchange can and should break down traditional bureaucratic boundaries. The question is whether we can expect this to happen in actual practice, and how technological opportunity shapes and is shaped by the socio-political contexts of actual public administration.

In this chapter, a case study of information sharing by means of information networks is presented. It provides an example of how information sharing can sometimes result in less benevolent practices, often referred to as 'data wars' or 'battles of the back office'.

The structure of this chapter is as follows. First, information networks are described as information resources or information assets. Various ownership structures (and thus, various levels of integration) will be described using political and economic organization theory. There follows a case study of the development of information networks in the Dutch research and development community. Finally, conclusions are drawn, and implications following from the social shaping of information networks are identified.

An economic and political view on information networks

Introduction

Chapter 4 has produced the advent of ubiquitous information sharing within and between organizations. In Chapter 4, the post-bureaucratic organization was introduced, and characterized as an organization in which bureaucratic control has imploded and given way to a form of control achieved through an integrated information infrastructure. In general, integrated information networks have great intuitive appeal. Although, from a technical point of view, inconsistent data semantics (for example, different definitions of performance criteria, coding schemes) may seriously obstruct workflows and day-to-day operations in networks of cooperating organizations. However, even in relatively unitary organizations that were aware of the problems associated with inconsistent data semantics and had attempted data standardization, integration failed or the organization experienced major difficulties (Goodhue et al., 1992; Shanks, 1997), for example because 'unwilling' local managers refused to give up control over information systems.

A political view on information networks

A political view (Davenport et al., 1992; Elg and Johanson, 1997) sheds some light on the background of the struggle surrounding information networks (Holland and Lockett, 1994; Kumar and van Dissel, 1996; Webster, 1995). In political organization theory, for example resource dependence theory (Pfeffer and Salancik, 1978), organizations inhibit a complex world, in which many of the resources needed to attain their goals (including information and knowledge, client referrals, money, legal authority, political legitimacy, people and equipment) are controlled by other organizations. This means that focal organizations enter into inter-organizational relations with partner organizations (for instance, by using information networks) in order to gain access to external resources. However, in doing this, they may have to comply with arrangements that have not been designed to suit them. Information handling procedures, terms of use and also data models may not always be geared to their requirements. In such a context, standardization of data models is certainly not a zero-sum game. According to political organization theory, each organization strives to optimize its self-interest by not only minimizing their dependence on other organizations but also maximizing the dependence of other organizations on themselves (Reekers and Smithson, 1996). Standardization can be used as a strategy by powerful organizations to deliberately affect the dependence between organizations in a way that favours them (Elg and Johanson, 1997). As Webster (1995) notes, standardization is an intensely political and adversarial process, because only the large and powerful parties can afford to get heavily involved in the standards development process. Truly joint design is therefore possibly a utopian ideal. As the less powerful parties are assumed to avoid further resource dependence, it is clear why the standardization of data models is often forcefully resisted. Otherwise the information networks are, in practice, sabotaged.

Case vignette 5.1: The politics of data modelling in the NHS

An example of information politicking is provided by Beynon-Davies (1994). He describes an attempt to develop a generalized model of healthcare data to be used in the British National Health Service (NHS). This can be characterized as a network of semi-autonomous organizations. Despite large efforts the data model was never actually implemented. Although the development of the data model was originally portrayed as a neutral and technocratic exercise, the participating organizations very actively opposed the data model because they felt that the data model, and especially the operational and financial data encompassed in the model, once implemented, could be used as a basis of comparison between NHS bodies. According to the semi-autonomous NHS bodies, the data model to be used to facilitate the exchange of information within the network raised unforeseen, partly unintended and very fundamental questions, about accountability within the network of cooperating organizations (in this case, the NHS: Beynon-Davies, 1994).

In a case study of a large, diversified organization, Markus (1983) reported that there was a suspicion that standardization of data models was used to enhance control over relatively autonomous divisions for the reason of 'ferreting out how the knaves were doing in the trenches' (Markus, 1983: 437). In a study of the diffusion of electronic data interchange technologies, Webster (1995) identified situations in which powerful organizations

> unilaterally imposed their in-house computer systems or information handling procedures upon their trading partners, extending their own hardware systems into their supplier's premises, dictating product and inventory coding according to their own established in-house information systems, and dictating the type and frequency of data to be exchanged.
>
> (Webster, 1995: 37)

Obviously, the view that networks of organizations can be regarded as structures containing mutual as well as conflicting interests (Elg and Johanson, 1997) also applies to the development and use of information networks (Reekers and Smithson, 1996).

Although political organization theory provides an explanation for the organization-political struggle surrounding the development and use of information networks, actors are usually less realistically depicted as aberrant managers or deviant technologists, focusing on political aspects, nurturing organizational autonomy and ignoring effectiveness and efficiency. The politicking in relation to information networks, however, is capable of being understood in other ways, among other things in ways that also include aspects of efficiency.

In order to show how a more sophisticated understanding could throw more light upon the topics under investigation, a body of knowledge complementary to political organization theory, namely economic organization theory (more specifically, property rights theory) is discussed below.

An economic view on information networks

Property rights theory (Bakos and Nault, 1997; Brynjolfsson et al., 1993; Van Alstyne et al., 1995) is an extension to standard neoclassical analysis (Homburg, 2001). It provides an analysis of behaviour of individuals with respect to assets (including information assets), under the assumption of bounded rationality. Bounded rationality refers to the impossibility to formalize all kinds of behaviour in contracts that encompass all future contingencies. Property rights theory is also referred to as incomplete contracts theory. If one regards information networks as information assets, it is possible to analyse behaviour with respect to these kind of information systems using property rights theory.

Property rights theory defines property rights as

> the sanctioned behavioural relations among men that arise from the existence of goods and that pertain to their use. These relations specify the norms of behaviour with respect to goods that each and every person must observe in his daily interaction with other persons, or bear the cost of non-observance
> (Furubotn and Pejovic, 1974: 3)

More specifically, Furubotn and Pejovich (1974) discern three categories of property rights: *usus*, the right to use an asset, *abusus*, the right to reconstruct an asset, and *usus fructus*, the right to appropriate the returns from the asset. If one regards an information system as an information asset, one can see that full ownership of these assets involves the right to use an information system, to modify it with quality-enhancing or cost-saving features, and to appropriate the benefits of these adaptations. As an owner may exert the *usus fructus* property right, it has intensive incentives to perform well.

One of the options an owner of an asset possesses is to allow others to use the assets in exchange for compensation, which may also be specified in a contract between user and owner. In this situation property rights theory states that because of bounded rationality, there will always be 'incompleteness' of contracts, implying that there will always be residual rights not covered in a contract. The institution that allocates these residual rights has ownership (Brynjolfsson et al., 1993) and hence, the owner is 'residual claimant'. This situation occurs when one organization, within a network of organizations, fully owns a central database while other organizations use it (that is, look in the database and/or enter information into the database) and contribute to the costs of the system through an agreed-upon lease contract. Such a separation of ownership and actual use has important consequences for behaviour pertaining to information assets. Think of an employee who is working with an information network that requires from him some specific investments, for example participation in an on-the-job quality improvement training programme. Such an employee faces intensive incentives to participate in a programme because in the long run, he can bargain for benefits in the form of a higher wage, promotion, more leisure time, and so forth. Consider the situation in which the system is owned by another organization, the marginal value of the participation of the employee in the programme can be expected to be divided among the employee, the boss and the owner of the system (as, in the bargaining process, the owner can exert hold-up power by threatening to withhold the asset). If the system were largely owned by his or her own organization, the owner can expect to receive a larger part of the marginal value in the bargaining process. Here we see that, in the absence of possibilities to formalize complicated reward schemes in contracts (e.g., assuming bounded rationality), a separation of ownership and control mitigates incentives. Van Alstyne et al. (1995) characterize this situation with the phrase 'rental cars are driven less carefully than cars driven by their owners'.

This situation is different in a number of specific situations, namely if one of the participants is indispensable or if assets are complementary. Complementary assets are assets that are useless when used separately but represent value when used in conjunction.

For the specific situation of information networks, it is relevant that the 'integration' of an information network mentioned before confronts employees with an attenuation of property rights. Hence, their incentives to perform well are partly mitigated. This mitigation of incentives results in subtle intangible costs of low effort which will eventually appear as distorted, missing, or unusable data. The line of reasoning can be summarized as follows: the more the sense of 'ownership' is diminished, the less intense incentives will be. Consequently, the level of investments in the information network will typically be lower, which in its turn affects the functionality, profitability, and eventually the viability of the information network. Of course, this line of reasoning is valid only in the absence of indispensability and complementarity of assets. In these cases, incentives of participants are best served by concentrated ownership, favouring participants' chances in ex-post bargaining processes.

Property rights theory applied to information assets provides a line of reasoning and a view on human behaviour which is arguably a caricature (as political organization theory does), but perhaps not such an unrealistic one. Combining economic organization theory and political organization theory, as we shall see below, provides us with a conceptual framework which allows the understanding of the difficulties and especially politicking surrounding the development and use of information networks.

Summary of the line of reasoning

In the introduction to this chapter, it was mentioned that there is a widely held belief among system developers and information managers that the more integrated information networks are, the larger the chance for success. After reviewing both political organization theory and economic organization theory, it is clear that integration, defined as the standardization of data definitions and data structures through the use of a common conceptual scheme across a collection of data sources, also has a number of negative consequences.

First, according to political organization theory, standardization of data definitions and data standards may be geared to the requirements of some organizations participating in an information network, but not necessarily to the requirements of all organizations. Integration, according to political organization theory, may be used to enshrine inter-organizational control and inter-organizational surveillance in information technology (Webster, 1995). This is supposed to be contrary to an organization's quest for autonomy.

Second, according to economic organization theory, standardization of data definitions and data standards can be conceived of as a mitigation of property rights with respect to the information system. Participants are less inclined to invest in the system and to enhance the information system with cost-saving or quality-enhancing features. Eventually such a diminishment of incentives results in less profitable, less functional and even less viable information networks. A typical symptom of lack of incentives is poor data quality, resulting from underinvestment in human and technical capital.

Following the line of reasoning set out in the previous sections, it is possible to hypothesize that in the absence of indispensability and complementarity of information assets, organizations will opt for disintegrated information networks where possible. This ensures that they can exert property rights with respect to the information networks (or parts of these) they are using. If we take the archetypes of the centralized database and the decentralized database with the referral index, we expect that cooperating organizations will prefer decentralized systems over centralized databases, which are fully 'owned' by one organization in a network of organizations that are using the system. This property theory line of reasoning, as well as a political view on information resources, contradicts the intuitive logic indicating that integration is a necessary precondition of the success of an information network. Indeed, it warrants other options than integration for these information systems.

In order to investigate this hypothesis, a case study of the exchange of information through an information network in the Dutch research community is presented in the following section. Before proceeding on to this case study, a brief note on research methods is appropriate. The case study employs diverse qualitative methods including interviews with information managers, system developers, administrators and users of information systems, observations and document analysis. Although this chapter draws principally from the case study presented here, it was also informed by two other case studies in the Dutch social security and fiscal policy sector. This case study illustrates and analytically generalizes novel theoretical ideas (at the cornerstones of information management theory, political organization theory and economic organization theory) that may be applied in varying contexts.

Case study: the development of information networks in the research community in the Netherlands

Background of the field and important stakeholders

As an introduction to the case study of the development and use of the NOD and CombiFormat inter-organizational initiatives, the policy and organizational background of the network under investigation should be first presented. In the Netherlands, an organizational network exists that consists of publicly or partly publicly financed research institutes. Traditionally, the Ministry of Education or, more specifically, the Directorate of Higher Education and Scientific Research, is an important player in the field. It provides financial support to research institutes and universities. The universities cooperate and participate in an interest association, the Association of Universities in the Netherlands (VSNU). The Royal Dutch Academy of Sciences (KNAW) is the interest association of the other research institutes.

Recently, the funding of institutes has changed from a hierarchical system towards a more a market-oriented system, in which institutes have a greater amount of autonomy. Administrators of research institutes concern themselves with their market share instead of lobbying government officials or predisposing the minister in favour of their plans. Historically, the institutes were used to report (initially in paper form and later on in the form of information systems) to a central registration owned by the Ministry. This implied that the Ministry requested information from the universities and research institutes and that the universities supplied the Ministry with the requested information. In fact, these information relations were, during the last few decades, stated in an information policy.

In 1985, research administrators quite explicitly opposed this approach, probably inspired by the changes in legislation (especially the system of funding) that were announced in that year. In the years before 1985, the information was used against them in cutback operations and the institutes, especially the universities, feared that these cutback operations would continue. During a discussion on information management organized by the interest association of the universities, an anonymous participant said: 'a couple of years ago, association measures were identified between input and output. Should we have the fox guard the chicken coop by means of automating our registrations?' In this case, the interest association of the Dutch universities presented its own information policy proposals, to be used in the network of universities, research institutes and government organizations. In 1990, it stated a number of information management principles, including that 'the information exchanged should match the informa-tion requirements of the institutes themselves'. Furthermore, the importance of exchange through formal reports is stressed and it is argued that the number of reports should be minimized. Finally, it is stated that 'controllability has to be sought in simplification rather than in integration of overly complex informa-tion flows' (VSNU, 1996: 5) and it is stated that 'there is no need for new, govern-ment-owned, centralized registrations' (VSNU, 1996: 5).

The 'Information Conference' of 1992 marked a change in the information management approach adopted for the exchange of information between research institutes and the Ministry of Education. The set of indicators used by the Ministry raised a lot of criticism. During the conference, the institutes agreed that they would be held accountable for their results according to a set of indicators, but they also managed to agree with the Ministry that the initiative for the formulation of these indicators would be primarily in the hands of the institutes and their associations. The institutes also acknowledged that the Ministry needs this information. However, there is a problem about the desired level of aggregation of the information to be exchanged. Agreement was reached on an approach in which the information needs of the Ministry will more and more be satisfied by the use of indicators.

Another very important result of the conference was that it was stated the Ministry of Education acknowledged that the information to be exchanged was owned by the research institutes.

Development of a research information system

A special topic in the exchange of information in the research community is the exchange of information on research activities. Registration of research activities was asked for in order to inform businesses, social organizations, international research organizations and government of the research projects that were being conducted by universities and research institutes. The importance of this kind of exposure of research activities, both nationally as well as internationally, is widely shared among the various participating organizations in the research community.

In order to accomplish this kind of exposure of research activities, in 1988, the NBOI was founded (this organization was renamed NIWI in 1997), among other things in order to design and develop a National Research Database (NOD).[1] This was also to be owned and maintained by the NBOI. The Ministry assumed that with the establishment of the NOD, with which the research institutes in principle had agreed, the universities were obliged to submit research information to the NOD. The VSNU, on the other hand, assumed that an obligation existed *only if* there was not a single trace of doubt as to not only the method of submission of information but also what organizations should eventually receive the information. In practice, the association wanted to postpone its commitment to the agreement until the results of the expected evaluation of the NOD were available and until its own investigation of the possibility of alternative approaches, in line with its own information policy statements, had been completed. The VSNU demanded complete freedom with respect to technical and organizational aspects, so that it is possible for them to align completely with their own information and management policies. In the meantime, there was a lot of quarrelling about who should provide the research information and who should contribute to the costs of the NOD. The latter question proved to be especially important because the institutes felt they did not receive any benefits from the NOD. Furthermore, the universities stated that they are not fully convinced of the usefulness of the [NOD]. ... The academic institutes are apprehensive of putting research information, which is to be classified as 'strategic' and which consists of input and output data at specific aggregation levels, at the disposal of (potential) users without explicit permission. If it is not clear to what use the information is to be put, [the institutes] refuse to supply this information.

Another participant stated that

if the NOD is accessible unconditionally, government is, through the back door, allowed access to information that, given the position of government, has to be characterized as 'management information'. Seen from the point of view of the universities, the supply of such an amount of management information is not acceptable.

In the proceedings of a discussion meeting, it was noted that there was a preference for a coordinating and referring function for the NIWI with respect to research information systems, and no need existed for a complete, central and uniform register with detailed information with respect to output of research activities.

At the same time, it was recognized that there were in practice problems with the day-to-day use of the NOD. Furthermore, a problem faced in the NOD initiative is that of the 14 universities, only 8 have had a contract with the database owner for electronic data interchange, and the filling of the database in general falls short of expectations.

In response to these developments, and, according to some stakeholders, out of sheer aggravation, the VSNU developed the CombiFormat data model, to be used as a basis for several research information systems. It is interconnected and separately owned by research institutes or groups of research institutes. In 1997, the CombiFormat was accepted and implemented by 10 of the 14 universities (Advantage, 1997), which had either developed a research information system (in Dutch: OZIS or OIS) themselves, or had bought an existing system which was developed by another research institute.[2] Although the federation of OIS/OZIS systems technically resembled the NOD database (in terms of design methodology, database technology, and so on), there was one crucial difference, the participating organizations were explicitly granted ownership of their OIS or OZIS systems. This allowed them for instance to adapt and modify the underlying data model, and, more importantly, allowed the research institutes (being *owners*) to exclude access to their data in cases where there was a suspicion of use which had not been agreed upon beforehand (for example in contingencies which had not been agreed upon in interchange agreements or other contracts with other research institutes, universities, the Ministry and NBOI/NIWI).

In the following period, two competing information networks existed. This occurred even though nearly all stakeholders agreed that the situation of competing information networks was not desirable and two expert opinions were asked for. In the experts' reports, it was first noted that if the parties involved do not succeed in increasing drastically the timeliness and coverage [of the NOD], it is not likely that a NOD-like structure will survive. And the former is a prerequisite for justifying the costs the NOD incurs.

(Wetenschappelijk Technische Raad, 1997: 8)

Furthermore, it is recommended to gather and enter data at the source as much as possible. In both reports, the necessity of a central database is questioned. In the report of the Wetenschappelijk Technische Raad, it is stated that possibly, over time, searches on decentralized databases could be a satisfying solution. In the Advantage report, the following is stated:

An important point of reference is that the organizations involved are highly autonomous. ... The choice of a specific approach therefore has to take these relationships and mutual interdependencies into account. Here, the relationships between institutes and between institutes and NIWI are at stake. A combined bottom-up/top-down approach, in which all participants are taken into account, is preferred. ... An incremental approach is to be preferred over a waterfall-like approach. ... It is furthermore important to notice that the relationship between NIWI and the institutes is not self-evident. This relationship will have to be nourished on the basis of mutual value-added.

(Wetenschappelijk Technische Raad, 1997: 9–10).

In general, both expert consultations resulted in support for the CombiFormat initiative and the OIS/OZIS systems over the NOD database. After an initial period of polarization, both the VSNU, research institutes and universities as well as the NBOI/NIWI supported the conclusions of the experts. Even the Board of the Royal Dutch Academy of Sciences, under whose heading the NBOI/NIWI formally operates, stated that it did not exclude the possibility that, over a certain period of time, the alternative of decentralized data storage would predominate. They noticed that the core of the report implies a changed role for the NOD, with a more important role for the decentralized input of data by the institutes which are responsible for the research activities.

Indeed the role of the NIWI changed from being a source of data (through the NOD), to an organization that focuses on quality assurance and the active (international) marketing of the research information owned by the research institutes and universities. Furthermore, the NOD itself has been transferred from being a 'pure' database to an information system with a variety of functions, of which the most important ones are the referral to OIS/OZIS system using a thesaurus of search terms and indices. This is in accordance with the participating organizations' preference for a coordinating and referring function for the NIWI.

Politics and property rights of NOD and CombiFormat

The developments mentioned above, relating both to the tasks and mission of the NIWI organization, as well as with respect to the NOD information system, marks the trajectory for changes in the research community in the Netherlands. Parts of these changes have already been completed and other changes are yet to come. Important for our analysis is that all stakeholders agreed that the centralized NOD system, fully owned by NIWI, is no longer an option, and that the decentralized OIS/OZIS systems are more viable.

From the perspectives of political and economic organization theory, a number of observations can be made. First of all, from within political organization theory, it can be seen that the research institutes and universities saw the establishment of the NOD as a sign of deliberate power use. More specifically, their fear was that the NOD could be used to gather management information, which could be used for other, strategic purposes, than merely registration of research information for national and international exposure of research activities. From the perspective of economic organization theory, the NOD represented an information asset to the participating institutes, which also elicited few incentives to invest scarce time and energy. In fact, the signs of underinvestment were present: the NOD suffered from poor data quality because not all institutes participated in the NOD and because the data that had been registered was neither timely nor accurate, and thus data quality was very poor.

The initiative to develop an alternative information network, undertaken by VSNU, can therefore be interpreted not only as a sign of 'sheer aggravation' but also as an attempt to develop an information system with more intense incentives to register data on research projects and eventually, to expose activities, nationally and internationally (a goal that is adhered to by many if not all participating institutes).

It is noteworthy that the crucial difference between the NOD and the OIS/OZIS system was not so much the technology nor the level of standardization as such (the CombiFormat data model of course was a de facto standard). Rather, the difference has to be sought in the dispersion of property rights. In the OIS/OZIS information systems, participating institutes were explicitly granted the right to *eventually* adapt the data model to local needs. Ultimately they had the capacity to exclude others from access to the databases, should there be suspicion of power abuse. Given the fact that the participating institutes were granted a high level of autonomy, the OIS/OZIS information systems provided them with far more intensive incentives to perform well, in terms of their maintenance of registration of research projects, than the centralized NOD system did.

Conclusions and discussion

The case study of an information network and its development in the Dutch research community demonstrated how the advent of ubiquitous information sharing through information technology can result in a 'battle of the back offices' or 'data war'. The development of the information network turned out to be a very political and adversarial decision making process. In the decision-making process, the influences of notions of incentives, underinvestment and attempts to avoid surveillance and control were observable. Furthermore, the study showed how a first attempt to develop an information network (that is, the NOD system) failed because its ownership structure did not match the characteristics of the network of organizations (in terms of autonomy of the participating institutes, incentives, and so on). An initiative to set up an (initially competing) information system with a more decentralized structure (CombiFormat), however, eventually replaced the NOD and became the information network to be used in the research community to record and exchange information on research endeavours.

The study therefore illustrates how important power, surveillance and control, incentives, as well as property rights are in the development of information networks. It is significant that the initially envisaged, integrated NOD system owned by NIWI did not in fact pass the evolutionary filter of efficiency and legitimacy in the network of organizations. It was replaced by an information system that was roughly based on the same kind of technology in terms of database technology and communication facilities, and yet it had a completely different ownership structure. This supports the idea that socio-political context (ownership structure and the behavioural consequences of ownership) shapes the information network as much as technological opportunity does.

This chapter has demonstrated that there is little support for the claim that a maximum level of informational integration across organizational boundaries is preferable. Although some participants in the network of research institutes saw the CombiFormat initiative as a sign of sheer aggravation, its emergence is perfectly understandable bearing the conceptual framework in mind. In fact, a line of reasoning encompassing economic and political aspects assumes prominence not only in the case description as a whole, but also by the anecdotal empirical evidence briefly mentioned in this chapter. Of course, it should be stressed that it is not suggested that the particular strategies employed by the organizations and actors in the network described in the case study are the most common or important ones. Nevertheless, these strategies were observed in the framework and may well arise in comparable situations.

Discussion questions

1   Explain why information is such a vital asset for many organizations, either in the private sector or in the public sector.
2   Name and explain an example of organizations striving to maintain and defend organizational autonomy.
3   Explain if (why) standardization is an adequate answer to the problems of hoarding and politicking as described in the case study.
4   What is the relevance of the political and economic logic set out in this chapter for the actual design of information systems?

Notes

1   NBOI is the Dutch Bureau for Research Information, or in Dutch, Nederlands Bureau voor Onderzoek Informatie (NBOI). On 1 September 1997, the NBOI merged with the Library of the Dutch Royal Academy of Sciences (Dutch abbreviation: BKNAW), the

Social Sciences Information Services (SWIDOC), the Dutch Historical Data Archives (NHDA) and the Bureau for Bibliography of Dutch Literature (BBN). The newly created organization, NIWI, is the new owner of the NOD, the Dutch Research Database. NIWI is an acronym for het Nederlands Instituut voor Wetenschappelijke Informatiediensten (The Netherlands Institute for Academic Information Services).

2 OZIS and OIS are two abbreviations for two local implementations of a research information system, or in Dutch, Onderzoeksinformatiesysteem.

References

Advantage (1997). *Oplossingsplan voor de VSNU inzake het WTR advies (Solution for the VSNU Concerning the WTR Report)*. Internal report. Rozenburg: Advantage and Utrectht: VSNU.

Bakos, J. Y., and Nault, B. (1997). Ownership and investment in electronic networks. *Information System Research, 8*(4), 321–341.

Beynon-Davies, P. (1994). Information management in the British National Health Service: The pragmatics of strategic data planning. *International Journal of Information Management, 14*(2), 84–94.

Brynjolfsson, E., Malone, T. W., Gurbaxani, V., and Kambil, A. (1993). Does information technology lead to smaller firms? *Management Science, 40*(12), 1628–1644.

Davenport, T. H., Eccles, R. G., and Prusak, L. (1992). Information politics. *Sloan Management Review, 34*(1), 53–65.

Elg, U., and Johanson, U. (1997). Decision making in inter-firm networks as a political process. *Organization Studies, 18*(3), 361–384.

Furubotn, P., and Pejovic, S. (1974). *The Economics of Property Rights*. Cambridge: Cambridge University Press.

Goodhue, D. L., Wybo, M. D., and Kirsch, L. J. (1992). The impact of data integration on the costs and benefits of information systems. *MIS Quarterly, 16*(3), 293–311.

Holland, C. P., and Lockett, G. (1994). Strategic choice and interorganisational information systems. Paper presented at the Hawaii International Conference on System Sciences (HICSS).

Homburg, V. M. F. (2001). The politics and property rights of information exchange. *Knowledge, Technology and Policy, 13*(3), 49–66.

Kumar, K., and van Dissel, H. G. (1996). Sustainable collaboration: Managing conflict and collaboration in interorganizational information systems. *MIS Quarterly, 20*(3), 279–300.

Markus, M. L. (1983). Power, politics and MIS implementation. *Communications of the ACM, 26*, 430–444.

Pfeffer, J., and Salancik, G. R. (1978). *The External Control of Organizations*. New York: Harper and Row.

Reekers, N., and Smithson, S. (1996). The role of EDI in inter-organizational coordination in the European automotive industry. *European Journal of Information Systems, 5*(2), 120–131.

Shanks, G. (1997). The challenges of strategic data planning in practice: An interpretative case study. *Journal of Strategic Information Systems, 6*(1), 69–90.

Van Alstyne, M., Brynjolfsson, E., and Madnick, S. (1995). Why not one big database? Principles for data ownership. *Decision Support Systems, 15*(4), 267–284.

VSNU (1996). *CIB-nota Informatiebeleid 1996*. Utrecht: VSNU.

Webster, J. (1995). Networks of collaboration or conflict? Electronic data interchange and power in the supply chain. *Journal of Strategic Information Systems, 5*(1), 31–42.

Wetenschappelijk Technische Raad (1997). *De Nederlandse Onderzoeksdatabank Nieuwe Stijl. Systeem voor Lopend Onderzoek Informatie.* Utrecht: Wetenschappelijk Technische Raad.

6 E-Government

A wired government takes shape

Key points

After reading this chapter, you will be able to

- define 'e-government' and explain the origins of e-government
- name and describe various types of e-government implementations (in terms of services and information relations that are triggered)
- identify similarities and differences (in terms of rhetoric) in various national e-government policies
- name implementation difficulties in e-government initiatives.

Introduction

In Chapter 1 a sketch was made of the way that the relatively new phenomenon of 'e-government' has confronted or actively engaged public administrations across the globe (Bekkers and Homburg, 2005; Chadwick and May, 2003; Fountain, 2001a, 2001b; Tat-Kei Ho, 2002). E-government refers to the strategic use of ICTs (especially Internet technologies, but also other kinds of ICT applications), in and around public administrations, for the purpose of creating a 'wired' or 'digital' government. Ideally, a wired government is more focused on and responsive to societal needs, it delivers services 24 hours a day, 7 days a week through information and communication technologies, and makes governments more efficient and democratic.

In practice e-government is also a very broad phenomenon. As Chadwick and May (2003) state: 'In the developed world, the Internet is now ubiquitous; government use of it is fast becoming so. For such countries, the issue is no longer whether government is online, but in what form and with what consequences' (Chadwick and May, 2003: 271). The concept of a wired government is defined and implemented in a variety of forms and shapes (Moon, 2002); this raises the question of how technology interacts with prevailing views on bureaucracy and democracy. As Dutton (1999) has stated:

> Digital government can erode or enhance democratic processes ... the outcome will be determined by the interaction of policy choices, management

strategies and cultural responses – not by the technology alone ... the debate over appropriate policies for guiding the application of ICTs in politics and governance needs to begin in earnest.

(Dutton, 1999: 193)

In this chapter, the concept of e-government is analysed including the technological, organizational and institutional reforms it frequently embodies, requires or coincides with. The chapter begins with a description of the origins of e-government. Then the variety in e-government services and the variety of roles that are envisaged for citizens in the context of e-government are described. National policies and their contents are sketched and then the actual manifestations and problems of e-government in practice are described. Conclusions are presented at the end.

Origins of a wired government

Introduction

E-government did not just emerge out of the blue. The popularity of e-government – either as a buzz word, or in actual practice – can be explained by a number of administrative trends and socio-political developments. These trends and developments are described below.

Re-engineering and the quest for citizens

Until about the 1970s, the concept of bureaucracy provided the uncontested organizational model for implementing policies. Since the 1980s, however, the concept of bureaucracy has been criticized for resulting in underperformance, inefficiency, and lack of responsiveness to needs and requests of citizens.

As a response to criticism, a new rhetoric of organizational and institutional change emerged in many countries, notably OECD countries. The apparatus of government had to become more customer-oriented, more responsive to societal needs, and to do that, governments had to take a more entrepreneurial position in society. It was said they had to *reinvent* and *reform* public administration to make this possible (Kettl, 2000). Many of the reforms were carried out by the name of *new public management*, which in essence implied that bureaucracies were to adopt leaner structures, market-like mechanisms, and a more active orientation towards citizens.

Since the 1990s, many politicians and policy makers have perceived ICTs as a means to *actually realize* and *further implement* the notions of administrative reform and new public management (see also Chapter 4). Most notable was the 1993 Clinton–Gore administration's 'Reengineering through Information Technology' which envisaged barriers of time and distance being overcome by electronic governance. It promised to give people information and services when and where they wanted them. Fostering citizen orientation has, in many countries, meant focusing upon the speed and efficiency of the administration, providing integrated digital access to government information and services, and, enabling intergovernmental tax filing, reporting, and payments processing (Tapscott, 1995). There have also been citizen-oriented communication initiatives and one-stop shops – which offer citizens physical or electronically shared service counters for, among other things, information, making complaints and submitting requests.

Case vignette 6.1: E-Government in Malaysia

Not only OECD countries, but also countries in the developing world are actually embracing e-government technologies. One example is Malaysia, which has embarked on the development of a technology park which stretches from Kuala Lumpur City Centre in the north to Kuala Lumpur International Airport in the south. This technology park is considered to be the nucleus of technological development, including e-government services and applications (which is in fact one of the seven pillars or flagships of innovation). The e-government flagship offers, among other things, Electronic Delivery Services (E-Services++), that enables online transactions between citizens, government and other providers of public services. Furthermore, Malaysia has implemented a Government Multi Purpose Card (MYKAD), a smart card that consolidates identification, licence, health and other information on one single card.

Opportunity: mimicking the dot-com bubble

Apart from administrative reform, there are other factors that can be used to explain the emergence and popularity of digital government. In the 1990s, Internet technology flourished and gave way to innovative business visions and actual models in which services were distributed through electronic networks, called e-commerce and then later e-business. Several years later, however, people began to talk about the dot-com bubble and toned down many of the previously lavish expectations of e-commerce and e-business. Nevertheless the idea was also noticed and embraced in the public sector, paving the way for some e-government initiatives. The emergence of e-commerce corresponded to prevailing ideas of administrative reform. In particular, because e-commerce was a technological private sector initiative, it gave further fuel to the idea that government could and should be run like a business. The technology, at least, was available to reform both the private, as well as the public sector.

Cleavage between government and citizens

A crisis in bureaucracy was already identified above as one of the reasons for reform. There are, however, other kinds of criticisms about governments and the public sector that go beyond supposedly inefficient and irresponsive public services. These include the view that the lack of service orientation has, in part, contributed to the frail condition of bureaucracy, but more significantly, has also had negative consequences for democracy as a whole. This broader conception of the frail condition of the public sector has led various authors to speak of a cleavage between the citizen and politics. It entails a situation in which citizens distrust politicians and civil servants, and where politicians are prone to elitism and do not represent the 'will of the people'. This cleavage can be seen as a fore-runner to a crisis in representative democracy (Bekkers and Zouridis, 1999; Bimber, 2003; Chadwick and May, 2003; Hague and Loader, 1999). In various countries, the cleavage between citizens and the administration has been addressed using a variety of strategies. One approach focuses primarily upon the administration itself and seeks to make it more citizen oriented. From the perspective of a crisis in democracy, however, this is seen to only scratch the surface of the cleavage problem. A second strategy goes somewhat further, and seeks to bring the administration closer to the citizen through increasing the (permanent) participation of citizens in the political and public debate. A lively democracy is not merely built on the number of people who actually vote in general, local and regional elections. A really 'strong' democracy should also embrace the idea of political debate and political action and should stimulate and facilitate citizens to raise their voice and be politically active. Strong democracy and 'active citizenship' are seen as two sides of the same coin. Interactive decision making and participatory planning processes are examples of this strategy, and it is striking that Internet technology can contribute to both.

Synthesis: e-government as technological, organizational and institutional redesign

The origins of e-government have been portrayed above. It has been shown that e-government is, at least to a certain degree, inspired by the proclaimed successes of e-commerce and e-business in the private sector. Technologies, and particularly the Internet, have been adopted to make governments and their administrations more citizen oriented. Through the application of network technology, the interaction between public administrations and their environments (including but not limited to citizens) have been significantly restructured. Some authors define e-government in a rather limited way, emphasizing or even limiting the concept to the idea of service delivery. For example, Norris and Moon (2005) define e-government as the electronic provision of information and services by govern-ments 24 hours a day, 7 days per week. However, if we look at the origins of the phenomenon, and the large variety of forms and shapes e-government initiatives take, it is probably more accurate to expand the definition. It needs to be recog-nized that e-government has redesigned the interaction between government and public administrations on the one hand, as well as the relationship of these bodies to all kinds of stakeholders (including citizens) on the other hand. Corresponding with this view, e-government has been defined as the redesign of information relationships between public administration and stakeholders in its environment in order to create some sort of added value. This can range from more efficient service delivery and more active citizenship strategies which seek to narrow the cleavage between government and citizens (Bekkers and Homburg, 2005; Bekkers and Zouridis, 1999).

Within the context and discipline of public administration, this view of e-government inevitably raises questions about who the citizen actually is or can be. It focuses attention on the kind of services that can be thought of in order to redesign the varying and conflicting demands of citizens. These issues are dealt with in the subsequent section.

Citizen roles and services

Citizen orientation: who is the citizen, anyway?

Many public administration reforms and e-government initiatives have been focused upon strengthening the relationship with citizens. In a context of public policy and public administration, the concept of citizen orientation is, however, highly problematic as the concept of citizen is a multidimensional one. One can distinguish many roles of the citizen in its relationship with government: customer, voter, taxpayer, applicant, *citoyen*, subject, stakeholder, civil servant (employee) and so on (Ringeling, 2001). Below, the concept of citizen is restricted to the roles of customer, *citoyen* and voter. A citizen can of course also be a customer of public services, but there are a number of striking differences from a customer in the market sector. Some are listed here:

- Many customers of public services are involuntary customers (in relation to, for example, prison services, tax payments and specific obligations).
- They cannot negotiate the price or quality of services when applying for services because generally the law forbids, hinders or, at least, does not stimulate government agencies to compete with one another on such matters as price, speed, quality or user friendliness.
- Once the right to a certain public service is established, public sector customers generally have an absolute right to delivery. This is because government agencies have a legal duty to ensure the delivery of the particular service. Unlike private enterprises, governmental agencies can seldom refuse delivery of the services and goods they have to offer in individual cases.

According to many authors, this does not imply that a customer orientation is irrelevant for public administration. Ringeling (2001), for example, argues that precisely because a citizen is not a voluntary customer, he or she needs to be treated with the utmost respect, especially because public services like taxation or speeding tickets usually do not translate into happiness of the citizen involved.

Case vignette 6.2: Electronic administrative supervision in the Netherlands

One of the initiatives of the Dutch government in relation to e-government is the development of so-called electronic inspectorates (under the heading of ICTU, a foundation established by the Ministry of the Interior and Kingdom Affairs for the purpose of generating and dispersing knowledge and best practices about ICT applications in the public sector).

Electronic inspectorates encompasses a variety of initiatives that are aimed at sharing information among inspectorates like the Labor Inspectorate, Food and Consumer Product Safety Authority and Tax Authority in such a way that the quality of inspection and site visits increases while the administrative burden for companies decreases.

Thus, this is an example of an e-government initiative in which it is attempted to make life better for citizens and companies that are involuntarily involved in the activities of government.

In the relationship between citizens and the democratic constitutional state, an important role of citizens is their position as *citoyens*. This role encompasses their activities as carriers of democratic rights on a more permanent basis. Referring to the notion of citizenship, a *citoyen* is an individual who participates in policy processes, political parties and social movements. In doing so, the individual exercises valuable democratic civil rights such as the rights to freedom of opinion and speech, to freedom of peaceful association and assembly, to demonstration and petition and – at least to some extent – the right of access to government information. For a long time, the role of citizens as bearers of democratic rights had been narrowed down to their role as voters. Nowadays, the role of the citizen as *citoyen* seems to be receiving renewed attention. This is a result of the decreasing importance of political parties and the growing individual involvement or political awareness in society. The Internet in particular has created many opportunities for supporting the citizen as *citoyen*. Worldwide access to government and other public information, or electronic debates and meetings, are just a few of the new opportunities that may contribute to individual involvement in various democratic processes in society.

E-Government services: types and levels of sophistication

In the previous section, the multifaceted character of citizen (and hence, citizen orientation) has been discussed. If one accepts that e-government applications can be used to foster customer orientation, then the consequence is that there is not one single type of redesign of information relationships that can be used to realize reforms (Bekkers and Homburg, 2005). The following types of services have been identified in practice:

- *Information services* are focused on the disclosure of government information, for instance the possibility of downloading brochures, policy reports, regulations and other official documents. Other examples include the possibility of searching in relevant databases or looking at benchmark information about the results of an agency.
- *Contact services* refer to the possibility of contacting government organizations. For instance, to ask questions of civil servants and politicians about the application of certain rules and programmes, or to make a complaint.
- *Transaction services* refer to the electronic intake and further handling of certain requests and applications of personal rights, benefits and obligations, such as digital tax assessments, the render of permits, licences and subsidies.
- *Participation services* address more than just the possibility of electronic voting. Electronic forums and virtual communities can provide citizens, interest groups and other parties a channel for getting involved in the formulation and evaluation of policy programmes. They may include the reconstruction of a neighbourhood, a shopping mall or the planning of a rail road.
- *Data transfer services* refer to the exchange and sharing of (basic and standard) information between government agencies and between government and private organizations.

In various countries, at various levels of government, instances of the above types of information provision are implemented. The degrees to which they are implemented, and choices for specific levels of sophistication, however, vary considerably. Chadwick and May (2003) state that it is not so much a question of technological 'maturity' that explains the type and level of information provision and/or interaction in the context of e-government initiatives, but moreover an underlying normative frame of reference. According to them, understanding e-government is not a question of understanding technology, but rather grasping the concept of democracy (see also Barber, 1997). Chadwick and May (2003) identify three models of interaction, with distinct normative roots and varying manifestations of specific electronic services:

- *A managerial model*, where there is a focus on administrative reform for the sake of efficient delivery of services to citizens, accurately targeted communication of citizen requests and faster responses. This model draws heavily on a reform agenda and on ideas stemming from *new public management*-like approaches. The assumption is that technology (including Internet technology) can help administrations to unilaterally deliver services to target populations, using for example the concept of Internet-based one-stop shops.[1] In order to serve citizens better, technology is being implemented not only in the communication between administration and its customers, but also within and between various government agencies. This promotes inter-operability and reduces the number of agencies that citizens must contact in order to complete a single request. In this model, there is a predominant focus on the citizen as a customer, and the type of services that are put in place to serve the citizen are primarily data and information services, and transaction services.

- *A consultative model*, in which technology facilitates the communication of citizen opinion to government. By utilizing technology, politicians and policy makers can swiftly sense the needs of 'real people'. Unlike the previous managerial model, this model includes some notion of participation and active citizenship. Although this is interpreted primarily in terms of promoting transparency with regards to citizens' needs and requests, and more responsive service delivery. It is less vocal about allowing citizens to have a bearing on policies or to have an actual political voice. The model focuses upon citizens as (empowered) customers and slightly as *citoyens*. It emphasizes both information and contact services, as well as some participation services.
- *A participatory model*, in which it is assumed that in order to craft policies for complex societal problems, citizens should be given access to government information and be allowed to (or even actively encouraged to) participate in policy making. Citizens are to share their views on the definition of collective problems and their proposed solutions, in an attempt to mobilise their support and creativity. To this extent, citizen involvement is also considered a means to improve policy making. In the participative model, interaction is regarded as constitutive of democracy itself. Democracy thrives on political discussion in forums and communities. The proliferation of virtual communities, online discussion forums, and a government that ultimately protects values of free speech and expression are supportive of this model. The model addresses the citizen primarily as *citoyen* and its primary focus is upon their participation in the design and delivery of services. These services, however, do not necessarily have to be provided by governments.

In general, one might infer that the type and sophistication of services in the context of e-government initiatives is shaped by the prevailing view on democracy. The degree to which this applies, is an empirical question. In the following section a number of national e-government policy initiatives are described and analysed, in order to illustrate some policy choices about e-government.

The rhetoric of a wired government in various countries

Introduction

E-government is, in many instances, a catchword, that is used in government debates, written language, and in consultancy to argue for reform, or to emphasize how reforms could actually be implemented. In order to reflect on the 'rhetoric' of the concept of e-government, one can analyse the language that is being used in government White Papers and policy documents. In doing so, the analysis takes place in a cultural, narrative sense, by *reading against* the assumptions embodied in policy documents (Bloomfield and Vurdubakis, 1994; Jensen and Lauritsen, 2005). In such an approach, e-government policies are regarded as *myths* (Edelman, 1967, 1977; March and Olsen, 1989; Mosco, 2004). Following Mosco (2004), I define myths as hymns to progress, and as utopian visions or promises unfulfilled or unfulfillable. It is important to state at the outset that myths mean more than falsehoods; rather, myths are used in this section not only as powerful stories that inspire people to strive for realization of issues that matter, whatever the cost (Buck-Morss, 2002), but also as discourses in which specific aspects are highlighted and revealed at the expense of other aspects that are (deliberately or unintentionally) concealed (Parsons, 1996). I assume that in order to reflect on the *rhetoric* of e-government projects, one should analyse the stories, or paths to transcendence, that inspire redesign of institutional arrangements (Mosco, 2004).

I do so by analysing the first waves (1994–2006) of e-government reforms, in which politicians and administrations embraced the transformative potential of ICT enabled projects. This was the period when Al Gore brought the notion of an information superhighway into the popular imagination. In the analysis, policy documents of the Netherlands, the United Kingdom, Denmark, Australia and Canada are scrutinized. In order to confront the rhetoric with the reality of e-government, I analyse a range of assumptions in the policy documents examined. First, I identify assumptions with respect to the goals and ambitions behind e-government initiatives. What claims are put forth to justify the actions and investments to be made? Second, I examine assumptions with regard to the assessment of the use and effects of ICTs. Such an assessment is of interest because ICTs are often seen as the most important means to modernization and institutional renewal. Third, I look at assumptions with respect to the barriers and problems that should be overcome. Very often these barriers reflect the major problems of government organizations, such as coordination and integration across agencies. We also examine the actions that policy documents stipulate should be undertaken for implementation of e-government initiatives. Given the barriers identified, how do governments act to put e-government into practice? The final set of assumptions examined concern the role of citizens. Most e-government initiatives are directed toward improving service delivery for citizens. How do citizens assess the possibilities of Internet technology in relationship to government? Are citizens portrayed as consumers or are they more than that?

Myth 1: a new and better government

The first myth eminent in the analysis of the various national policy documents is the purified image of a new and better government. In such a reformulated government, ICTs are seen as helping the realization, with little effort, of administrative machinery that is responsive, client-oriented and cohesive.

In the UK documents *Modernising Government* (Minister for the Cabinet Office, 1999), *E-Government: A Strategic Framework for Public Services in the*

Information Age (Minister for the Cabinet Office, 2000) and *Transformational Government* (Minister for the Cabinet Office, 2005), e-government is seen as having only one purpose: to make life better for citizens and businesses. The focus upon the *improvement* of electronic service delivery assumes that it will deliver what people really want, fully exploiting government's information resources.

Case vignette 6.3: Electronic service delivery in the UK

In the UK, the wording of policy initiatives emphasizes electronic service delivery, transparency and ease of access: 'new technology offers the
possibility of making access to information about government easier . . . .
The digital age also offers the possibility of a better informed and more
participative democracy through electronic consultation and better
responses to feedback' (Minister for the Cabinet Office, 2000: 8). In
Transformational Government, the promise of a new and better government is stretched further: 'The specific opportunities lie in improving
transactional services . . ., in helping front line *public servants* to be more
effective . . ., in supporting effective *policy outcomes* . . ., in reforming the
corporate services and *infrastructure* which government uses behind the
scenes' (Minister for the Cabinet Office, 2005: 3; emphases in original).

In the UK vision emphasis is on the notion of intra-governmental cooperation: 'To improve the way we provide services, we need all parts of the government to work together' (Minister for the Cabinet Office, 1999: 4).

Australia's *Government Online: The Commonwealth Government's Strategy* (Department of Communications Information Technology and the Arts, 2000) articulates the goal as improving the quality of all public services, and increasing responsiveness of public service delivery. *Government Online* is the natural extension of the emphasis on service quality and meeting the needs of clients, which has already been put forward in previous reports, such as *Investing in Growth* (Department of Communications Information Technology and the Arts, 1997). In this specific document, the goal of putting all appropriate government services online by 2001 was established. Moreover:

> Government Online will contribute more broadly to service quality beyond
> just the impact on individual agencies and their service charters. Online tech-
> nology has the potential to break down traditional barriers faced by clients.
> (Dept of Communications Information Technology and the Arts, 2000: 5)

In the 2006 Australian policy document *Responsive Government*, there is also reference to a technologically enabled, seamless governmental apparatus:

> It will be possible to group diverse transactions and complete them at
> the same time, without navigating the underlying structure and complexity

of government. People will be able to interact with many areas of government without needing to understand exactly which agencies deliver which services.

(Department of Finance and Administration, 2006: 8)

The mission of the Canadian e-government policies, as formulated in the *Government Online* programmes (Treasury Board, 1999, 2000, 2006) is to advance the federal government's citizen centred service delivery vision collaboratively across departments and other levels of government.

In the Danish vision on e-government *From Vision to Action: Info-Society 2000* (Ministry of Research and Information Technology, 1995), e-government is described, conceptualized and discussed in the context of the network society: a worldwide short circuit of time, space, people and processes. As such, the Danish case (at least until 2004) is an exceptional case in the sense that ICTs are seen as contributing to free access of information, grassroots democracy, personal development of individuals in workplace and private life, and transparency of the administrative apparatus:

> The new technologies must give all citizens free access to information and exchange of information, and the possibilities for increasing the citizens' self determination are to be exploited. It must be ensured that the technologies are not used for monitoring citizens or invading their privacy.
>
> (Ministeriet for Videnskab Tecknologi og Udvikling, 2000: 9)

In order to accomplish the goals described above, policy makers put emphasis on lifelong learning, the stimulation of e-commerce, more effective and cheaper public service delivery, the stimulation of grassroots digital democratic initiatives, and the establishment of information intensive organizations in specific regions (so-called IT lighthouses). The above vision of e-government contrasts with that of the 2004 policy document *The Danish eGovernment Strategy 2004–06* (Digital Taskforce, 2004). In this document the vision is articulated in one sentence: 'digitalization must contribute to the creation of an efficient and coherent public service with a high quality of service, with citizens and businesses in the centre' (Digital Taskforce, 2004: 4).

In the Netherlands, *Action Program for Electronic Government* (Ministry of the Interior and Kingdom Relationships, 1999) and *The Digital Delta* (Ministry of Economic Affairs, 1999) present the goals of e-government as increasing the accessibility of government, improving the quality of public services, and enhancing the internal efficiency of government. They see e-government as a vehicle for getting the Dutch government to actively focus on its role as producer of public services. In a subsequent document, *Contract with the Future* (Ministry of the Interior and Kingdom Relationships, 2002), the scope of e-government is broadened: the political participation by citizens is identified as an area that deserves stimulation.

If one scrutinizes the major barriers that obstruct the realization of e-government objectives, one can observe a wide variety of barriers noted in the texts, including:

- the absence of inter-operability and (technical) standards (Treasury Board 1997)
- agencies fostering local interests at the expense of citizens' interests (Minister for the Cabinet Office, 1999)
- a decentralized approach to ICT development (Minister for the Cabinet Office, 1999)
- inability to redefine working routines and develop new ICT-based products (Digital Taskforce, 2002).

We see that a new and better government is rhetorically crafted in the wordings of the various policy documents. This new and better government is seen as acting as a whole or joined up, as per the British jargon. Technology is seen as playing a decisive role not only in the actual achievement of a joined-up administrative apparatus (and thus, in the redefinition of information relations with internal stakeholders, see pp. 90–91) but also in realizing online transactions between government on the one hand, and citizens and businesses (external stakeholders) on the other hand.

Each of the countries that were studied tries to establish citizen or business centric one-entry points. However, the goal of integrated electronic service delivery – especially in relation to contact and transaction services – leads, in practice, to serious integration and coordination problems. Integrated service delivery implies that several back offices should work together in handling questions, requests and so on. They need to share information and knowledge across internal and external organizational boundaries. In essence, the exchange and sharing of information and knowledge between these back offices implies the integration of several information domains, each with its own legal framework, its own information systems, its own data definitions, its own routines and procedures, its expertise and experience, and its own frames of reference (Bellamy and Taylor, 1997; Homburg, 1999, 2000). The cooperation of the back offices and integration of different information systems and policies implies that positions and interests will have to change (Homburg and Bekkers, 2002). Thus, ICT is not only a source of innovation but also a source of resistance or even what is referred to as a 'battle of the back offices' (Homburg, 1999; Knights and Murray, 1992; Kraemer and King, 1986; Kraemer et al., 1987; Kumar and van Dissel, 1996). This battle is the Achilles heel of e-government. An examination of recent assessments of the e-government initiatives in general (Gartner, 2000; OECD, 2003), and the assessments of e-government practices in the Canada, the UK, Australia and the Netherlands show that the lack of cooperation between these back offices is still a major problem. In a Dutch study on inter-organizational electronic service delivery, Van Venrooij (2002) has shown that the most important impediments to integration are coordination problems due to an ambiguous distribution of tasks and legally defined competences among the back offices. While these offices should be working together, the plurality of the actors and interests at stake, together with the lack of a common vision or *sense of urgency* about the necessity to work together, prevent cooperation. Similarly, a focus on service delivery structures instead of a focus on the processes of service delivery or the incompatibility of data systems and data definitions prevent the desired integration. Remarkably, if the integration problems of the back offices are addressed in various e-government policy documents, it is primarily and predominantly articulated as a technical problem for which a technical solution exists (OECD, 2003). It is rarely seen as a problem of institutional design, that is, in terms of actors, their interests, their power bases and resources, their relationships and their strategies, conflict and compromises (Homburg, 1999).

Myth 2: the myth of technological progress and instrumentality

In the UK the various promises of ICT are written in the imperative: 'ICT will . . .', for instance 'make our life easier' (Minister for the Cabinet Office, 1999: 7). Similarly, in the UK *Transformational Government* White Paper, the use of technology is described as 'creating and retaining the capacity and capability to innovate and use technology effectively as technology itself develops' (Minister for the Cabinet Office, 2005: 4).

ICT as an *exogenous* driving force is also evident in Danish documents. Introducing the Internet, the authors of the Danish policy document *From Vision to Action: Info-Society 2000* speak of a network-like environment which is not amenable to government control. Consequently, the information society is seen as developing into an open and decentralized society: 'The numerous global networks with their debates, databases and dissemination of information do not lend themselves to control. They invite both anarchy and refreshing debates' (Digital Taskforce, 2002: 4). In general the Danish see the information society as a revolution in progress that cannot be missed. The only question is how to respond to it.

Dutch programmes like *The Digital Delta* (Ministry of Economic Affairs, 1999) and *Action Program for Electronic Government* (Ministry of the Interior and Kingdom Relationships, 1999) show a strong belief and trust in the potential of modern ICT. Optimism prevails about the progress ICT will bring.

In Australia's *Government Online* (2000), there is hardly any sphere of activity that could not be improved by online government – to achieve more, and to do it more quickly and efficiently. Online access to information is seen as having a significant impact on regional communities, older Australians and people with disabilities. Online service delivery is seen as complementing and replacing existing traditional service channels and providing around the clock access to government from almost everywhere, breaking down the barriers of distance or mobility that some clients face.

The Canadians also see a changing landscape in which distance perishes and a picture of ubiquitous computing dawns. ICT infiltrates almost every aspect of modern life, resulting in the rise of a new set of expectations and demands. People have nomadic access to their information and computing systems from publicly shared access points. ICT allow us to imagine new ways of connecting citizens, of eliminating the barriers of distance, and of giving a fuller, richer meaning to democracy and citizenship.

In the various national policy documents, there is a strong belief and trust in the potential of ICTs. Optimism prevails in the descriptions of the progress the information society and Internet technology will bring. Things that were previously unthinkable will now happen. Public administration has a moral duty to use the most advanced 'tools' to reinvent government. The dominant view of technology that is exhibited in several of the policy documents is a selective combination of determinism and voluntarism. Both positions are brought together by the assumption that the emergence of the information society coincides with technologies whose potential cannot be denied.

Using existing reflections on the use of ICTs in organizations (Bellamy and Taylor, 1997; Bijker et al., 1981; Snellen and van de Donk, 1998), however, it is possible to question the generic effects of ICTs. Often, effects are specific and context-dependent, and in the policy documents studied, political, socio-organizational and institutional settings are hardly mentioned or paid attention to. These effects are limited and context-dependent because the introduction of ICT in public administration is a social intervention in a policy and organizational network, which influences the position, interests, values and (information) domains of the actors involved. Thus, the introduction and use of ICT is not a neutral, but a political intervention (Homburg, 1999; Kling, 1987). ICT in the public sector very often strengthens the existing frames of reference, power relations, and positions within a policy sector (Bekkers, 1998; Kraemer and King, 1986; van de Donk, 1998; Zuurmond, 1998). Assuming this is not so, can be regarded as another myth: a myth of (unquestioned and ubiquitous) material and technological progress.

Myth 3: the myth of e-government as rational information planning

In the documents that were studied, a picture emerges in which application of ICT tools (in the right way) is seen as a precondition for institutional renewal. For instance, in the Canadian e-government documents four priorities to stimulate a smooth implementation of e-government are identified: aligning various ICT-infrastructures, developing a world class ICT workforce within government, the improvement of the management and success rate of ICT investments, and the minimizing of risks of ICT projects. In the Danish strategy, collaboration between the private and public sector is seen as a necessary condition for Denmark's transition toward the Information Society. The focus is on implementing a relatively small number of projects with realistic goals and clear deadlines. In Australia's *Government Online*, a national approach to e-government is promoted based upon a number of priorities: a systematic approach to placing its information and services online, relevant enablers (i.e. authentication, privacy and security), the development of transaction and payment services, and cross-agency collaboration. In Dutch accounts of electronic government, there is an emphasis upon the establishment of virtual services counters, which are theme-oriented, such as 'living and building', 'care and welfare', 'companies', and on the reduction of 'administrative costs for companies'.

When we compare the initiatives across countries we see that the primary focus is on the use of rational planning and management methods to accompany the introduction of ICT. Only the Danes chose an incremental approach, the Dutch paid no attention, in the documents we studied, to an implementation strategy. The secondary focus is on the development of all kinds of technological applications that should be developed and deployed.

In the UK, Australian and Canadian documents, corporate information planning and project management techniques are seen as intrinsic to the e-government project. The path forward is presented as a question of setting goals, formulating action plans, allocating budgets, and identifying clear roles and responsibilities. A number of technocratic assessments of the practice of e-government (Accenture, 2002; OECD, 2003), identify pitfalls in the effective implementation of e-government, such as bad planning and bad project management.

In the scholarly literature two serious questions have been raised about such an approach (Ciborra, 2002; Gazendam, 1993; Mason and Mitroff, 1981). First, the actual practice of ICT planning and implementation does not always reflect the systematic methods and procedures of information systems management models. ICT-driven innovations in private and public organizations are mostly the result of the bubbling up of new ideas from the bottom (Ciborra, 2002; Homburg, 1999). Second, formulating and implementing e-government can be viewed as a governance problem that takes place in the context of a network of organizations. On the one hand, standardization and integration in the back office is needed to allow for inter-organizational information exchange, while on the other hand standardization and integration may intensify existing dependencies and enshrine these dependencies in the technology (Ciborra, 2002; Homburg, 1999; Homburg and Bekkers, 2002). Consequently, excessive integration fuels inter-organizational tensions and conflicts.

The fact that in various documents, the downside of integration and standardization are ignored, and strategic planning practices are heralded, gives rise to another myth: the myth of rational information planning.

Myth 4: the myth of citizen as empowered consumer

In many policy documents the citizen is portrayed as an intelligent and 'empowered' consumer, while government is presented primarily as a service organization. For instance, a UK report notes, 'People are aware of the possibility and benefits of excellent service, and they expect it in all dealings with business. . . . The challenge for the public sector is that the same growing expectations will be applied to government services' (Minister for the Cabinet Office, 2000: 8). Similarly, according to an Australian report, an online environment will allow individuals to customize their online channel with government, to make it more useful, familiar, convenient, and in many instances, transparent. The government should facilitate this by 'bringing government closer to people to encourage people to interact with government' (Department of Communications Information Technology and the Arts, 2000: 7).

Although all the documents analysed recognize, at least to some degree, intelligent, technologically empowered citizens-as-clients, two types of refinements can be observed.

First, the notion of citizens as mere customers is modified in the Canadian e-government thinking: they are portrayed as playing the role of good citizens (Schudson, 1998). In this role, citizens are allowed and even encouraged to speak up and participate (electronically) in the democratic process.

Second, the notion of the omni-rational consumer (who knows his or her preferences, is able to master both bureaucratic as well as ICT skills and actively engages in conversation with government agencies) is refined in the Danish e-government document, in which attention is paid to the increased social polarization into a two-tier society with ICT winners and ICT losers. The Danish report proposes the use of ICT to support the personal development of the citizen and to give individuals the opportunity to exercise their influence to speak up: 'Individuals must, themselves, demonstrate their constructive interest in the potential of the info-society and avail themselves of opportunities in the educational system, public libraries, et cetera' (Ministeriet for Videnskab Tecknologi og Udvikling, 1996).

It must be noted, however, that the somewhat enlightened vision of citizens in the Danish documents until about 2000 is abandoned in subsequent documents (Digital Taskforce, 2002, 2004; Ministeriet for Videnskab Tecknologi og Udvikling, 2000) (see also Myth 1).

In other words, the multifaceted and somewhat enlightened vision on citizens seems to have become narrowed down to the notion of a consumer of public services.

In the Netherlands, the emphasis is also upon the citizen as a consumer of government services. In *Contract with the Future*, a relationship between the rise of the empowered and intelligent citizens and the process of individualization is identified. These new citizens demand a government which is responsive to their needs, able to generate an open and horizontal dialogue, and organize its internal processes in a transparent way.

We thus see that the dominant image of the citizen is that of someone who acts as and should be approached as a consumer. It is only in the Canadian and Dutch documents that attention is drawn to the democratic and participatory role of citizens, but still the emphasis remains primarily upon the consumer role of citizens.

The image of an intelligent citizen, who uses the possibilities of the Internet in optima forma to improve his or her position as a consumer of government services is dominant across the documents. It is assumed that citizens will demand a public administration that also uses the possibilities of the Internet in optima forma; a public administration which enables them to act as empowered and intelligent citizens. These assumptions about the role of the citizen and government are not without risk.

Fountain (2001a, 2001b) points to the so-called legitimacy paradox of public service delivery. In her view, the improvement of the quality of public service delivery paradoxically does not increase the legitimacy of government; rather, addressing citizens as consumers and defining government as a production company ignores the public and political character of service delivery. A focus on service delivery (and a focus on the consumer rather than on the citizen) narrows the multidimensionality of citizenship and public administration and may therefore decrease legitimacy. The challenge for e-government is to develop participative forms of electronic service delivery and to address citizens at the same time as their identities as consumer, voter and a Good Citizen or *citoyen*.

Synthesis: blended initiatives

In the previous section I briefly sketched national policies regarding e-government. Given the range of interactive behaviour in the context of administration-citizen relationships, two observations can be made.

First, the full range of possible interactions (managerial, consultative and participatory) is not reflected in any of the national policies discussed. In general, all national policies mention or mirror a managerial approach towards e-government, emphasizing the need for information services and especially transaction services and data services (for the sake of electronically integrating public administration, so that citizens do not have to be asked repeatedly for the same information over and over again and that agencies and ministries can truly cooperate and share information). It seems that e-government is indeed viewed as a set of technological means that can be put to use to realize the idea of administrative reform and to make new public management work.

Second, it is striking that the national policies differ considerably with respect to the degree to which some of the elements of consultative and participatory models are included in the accounts of interaction between the administration and citizens. The UK and the USA barely referred to consultation and participation in their e-government policies, whereas the Danish approach in particular made direct references to more consultative interaction between the administration and citizens.

Of course, this does not imply that electronic consultation and participation does not exist in the UK and in the USA, nor does it imply that in Denmark and the Netherlands electronic consultation and participation necessarily flourishes. Chadwick and May (2003), for example, mention various successful US e-government projects in which electronic participation has been realized. Inversely, the implementation of participatory and consultative services in all countries surveyed, including the Netherlands and Denmark, raises many questions and results in many problems. These problems of practice, however, are distinct from policy statements and ideas (or rhetorics). They are concerned with the reality of a wired government at the shopfloor of e-government. This issue is dealt with in the next section.

The reality of a wired government in various countries

Introduction

In the previous section, goals and objectives of national e-government policies were described. This, however, does not necessarily say anything about actual e-government practice. Implementation of e-government initiatives is known to be a complex process, and in implementation processes shifts in emphasis occur frequently. In this section, studies of existing e-government practices are presented in order to reveal at least some actual e-government practices.

National sophistication results in Europe

The European Union (more specifically, the Directorate General for Information Society and Media) regularly surveys online presence of public services in its member states. According to a 2004 survey, online presence of public service providers in various countries in Europe range from 78 per cent (for the 10 new member states) to 87 per cent (for the 18 other states) (European Commission Directorate General for Information Society and Media, 2005). The sophistication of web presence, however, falls short of presence as such: 40 per cent of public services are fully transactional online. Online sophistication (i.e., measured by a scale which indicates information services, unilateral communication, bilateral communication, and transaction services) is the most advanced in Sweden, Austria, UK, Ireland, Finland, Norway and Denmark. Full transaction services are offered best in Sweden, followed by Austria and Finland.

An important finding in the survey is that there is a large gap between online development of income generating services (tax payments, contributions from citizens and corporations to the government) and other services. Income generating services reach a level of 88 per cent throughout European member states, as opposed to administrative obligations that score far below average.

In conclusion, it is possible to state that in the various countries, throughout various levels of government, more and more information is published online, yet the majority of services are strictly informational. Within the domain of the managerial model of interaction, only a minority of services are offered on a fully transactional basis. In the report, various reasons are given that might explain this observation (European Commission Directorate General for Information Society and Media, 2005):

- issues with respect to security have to be dealt with before transactional services can be put online
- lack of coherent national e-government policies that guide local developments
- the state moving away from being a direct supplier of public services to a regulator of the way quasi-autonomous agencies and private companies provide public services.

Paradigm shifts in American city websites

Several surveys have been conducted to assess the actual e-government situation in US local governments. Alfred Tat-Kei Ho (2002) surveyed paradigmatic transitions from traditional functionally differentiated bureaucratic organizations to citizen-oriented service agencies in US local governments. He did so by analysing city websites and their underlying portal designs. These could either be administrative oriented, information oriented or user oriented. Administrative-oriented portals provide information that is organized primarily according to the administrative structure of bureaucracy and does not reflect any kind of rethinking of public service delivery. The information-oriented design, on the other hand, offers tremendous amounts of information, albeit without categorizing information according to bureaucratic (departmental) logic. The user-oriented design of portals goes one step further by categorizing information according to the needs of specific user groups.

Tat-Kei Ho (2002) analysed web portals of 55 of the most populous cities in the United States. It was concluded that most cities had transformed their web presence from an administrative-oriented portal design (reflecting bureaucratic logic of a variety of functionally differentiated departments) to informational- and user-oriented portals. Furthermore, responses by city web masters indicated that many city officials had abandoned a departmental mentality in web management. The 55 surveyed city web portals predominantly reflected service orientation, and although many cities actively sought citizens' input on how they should design websites and deliver services online, only a few cities engaged citizens in online policy dialogues or partnered with community organizations to strengthen participation (Tat-Kei Ho, 2002).

On the basis of two surveys among local governments at a local level, Donald Norris and Jae Moon (2005) concluded that public administration is making progress in adopting and employing e-government technologies. This progress is most visible in the number of websites providing service delivery, but it is not yet evident in website sophistication. Most websites offer informational services, but no transaction services; and they display predominantly departmental, bureaucratic logic rather than horizontally and vertically integrated services.

Conclusion

E-government, a relatively new phenomenon, has been introduced in this chapter. It can be defined as the redesign of information relationships between administration and citizens, in order to create some sort of added value. The origins of e-government can be found not only in motives for cost-cutting, but also in the realization of new public management-type of reforms (making public administrations more citizen oriented, efficient, transparent and responsive to the needs of the public). Moreover, an important stimulus for e-government is to bridge the gap between administration and citizens, and to address the so-called democratic deficit or cleavage between government and citizens.

Many authors have proposed ways to redesign various types of interaction between government and administration on the one hand, and the roles of citizens on the other hand. In practice, various implementations of e-government can be envisaged, ranging from data services (agencies mutually exchanging and sharing information), information services (for example, putting brochures online), transaction services (allowing citizens to fully complete requests, ideally without having to repeatedly submit information to various agencies involved in the request), and participation services (allowing for online debates on policies).

A number of observations have also been made about the implementation of e-government. First, in national e-government initiatives, there seems to be a preference for a managerial connotation of e-government, irrespective of whether the emphasis is on integrated service delivery to citizens and corporations. This reflects a managerial or new public management-like orientation to the redesign of information relationships. Especially in the Anglo-Saxon countries, e-government is predominantly seen as 'e-business for governments', and scarce references are made to the potential of Internet technologies for consultative and participatory services. While the citizen role of *citoyen* is absent from these documents, it is the view of citizens as customers of public services that predominates.

Second, if one looks at actual implementation of e-government in both the local administration of the United States and in national and local administrations in the European member states, one can conclude that many, if not the majority of public agencies, have websites (so the web presence of government is fairly high). They also reflect an increasing focus upon citizen (or rather customer) orientation. However, actual citizen orientation requires more than redesigning ways in which ('external') communication takes place within the administration on the one hand, and between the administration and citizens on the other hand. There are at least two barriers preventing actual and true citizen orientation. The first is that many services are informational and not (yet) transactional. The second major barrier, preventing many citizens from receiving the services they require, is that traditionally, many public organizations have been used to approaching citizens according to their own bureaucratic and institutional logic. This is significantly different from an approach that focuses upon the needs and requirements of individual citizens and corporations.

Or to put it another way service delivery has typically been supply oriented rather than demand driven. To make things worse for citizens and corporations, many requests require actions from multiple agencies, and a highly compartmentalized public administration does not make it easier for citizens to get what they need or require. It becomes clear that innovative service delivery will not flourish from ICT application alone. In addition, integrated service delivery (using a one-shop-no-stop model) is needed, which in its turn requires public organizations to gear their internal processes towards the requirements of citizens and corporations. They also must cooperate and exchange information with other government bodies involved in service delivery. Obviously, there is a world to be won behind the virtual front office, since it is in the so-called back office where various agencies and departments have to cooperate, share and exchange information in order to complete citizens' requests.

E-government application is shaped predominantly by a specific model of interaction between citizens and administration, the managerial model. Many if not most e-government initiatives are focused on electronic delivery of public services to corporations and citizens in their role as 'customers'. Consistent with the conceptual frame of reference that is used in this book, one can conclude that the predominant managerial model shapes and filters types of technological innovations that are being put into practice. As Chadwick and May (2003) conclude: there is *a fortiori* nothing wrong with the managerial model's notion of the citizen primarily as a consumer of public services, and many citizens might benefit from improved, integrated public service delivery by more efficient, more transparent and more responsive public administrations. There is, however, a compelling argument against too narrow a focus on public service delivery and this argument has been developed by Jane Fountain (2001a, 2001b). She claims that in principle, with improved public service delivery, politicians and policy makers attempt to bridge the gap between citizens and the administration. However, the more e-government initiatives primarily focus on service delivery, the less justice is paid to the specific, multifaceted character of public administration, thereby eventually and paradoxically decreasing legit   of these institutions. This line of reasoning makes a compelling case for recognizing the multifaceted character of government in e-government initiatives. It should encompass not only a managerial model of interaction between administration and citizens, but also consultative and participative models.

Discussion questions

1 Sometimes, e-government is defined as 'e-commerce for government' or 'e-business for government'. To what degree do you think this is a valid definition? In what respects is e-government, as depicted in this chapter, different from 'e-commerce' or 'e-business'?

2 Explain why some e-government initiatives focus on service provision, whereas others emphasize participation.

3 To what degree do you think various national e-government policies converge in terms of formulation of aims, implementations, and so on?

4 Why do you think e-government often takes the form of electronic service delivery?

Note

1 One-stop shops or one-stop service centres are not new. The idea had already emerged in the 1970s and 1980s. By then, one-stop shops required massive reorganizations and rearrangement of authorities and responsibilities. E-government one-stop shops employ technology to bridge functionally differentiated organizational units without massively reorganizing organizations; by avoiding reorganizations, this type of one-stop shop is less likely to end in bureaucratic resistance in implementation (Tat-Kei Ho, 2002).

References

Accenture (2002). *E-Government Leadership: Realizing the Vision*. Retrieved from www.accenture.com June 2006.

Barber, B. (1997). The new telecommunications technology: Endless frontier or the end of democracy. *Constellations*, 4, 208–228.

Bekkers, V. J. J. M. (1998). Wiring public organizations and changing organizational jurisdictions. In I. T. M. Snellen and W. B. H. J. van de Donk (eds) *Public Administration in an Information Age*. Amsterdam: IOS Press.

Bekkers, V. J. J. M, and Homburg, V. M. F. (eds) (2005). *The Information Ecology of E-Government*. Amsterdam: IOS Press.

Bekkers, V. J. J. M., and Zouridis, S. (1999). Electronic service delivery in public administration. *International Review of Administrative Sciences*, 65(2), 183–195.

Bellamy, C., and Taylor, J. (1997). Transformation by stealth: The case of the UK criminal justice system. In J. Taylor, I. T. M. Snellen and A. Zuurmond (eds) *Beyond BPR in Public Administration*. Amsterdam: IOS Press.

Bijker, W. E., Hughes, T. P., and Pinch, T. J. (eds) (1981). *The Social Construction of Technological Systems*, Cambridge, MA: MIT Press.

Bimber, B. (2003). *Information and American Democracy: Technology in the Evolution of Political Power*. Cambridge: Cambridge University Press.

Bloomfield, B. P., and Vurdubakis, T. (1994). Re-presenting technology: IT consultancy reports as textual reality constructions. *Sociology*, 28(2), 455–477.

Buck-Morss, S. (2002). *Dreamworld and Catastrophe: The Passing of Mass Utopia in East and West*. Reading, MA: MIT Press.

Chadwick, A., and May, C. (2003). Interaction between states and citizens in the age of the Internet: 'E-Government' in the United States, Britain, and the European Union. *Governance*, 16(2), 271–300.

Ciborra, C. (2002). *The Labyrinths of Information*. Oxford: Oxford University Press.

Department of Communications Information Technology and the Arts (1997). *Investing in Growth*. Canberra: Department of Communications, Information Technology and the Arts.

Department of Communications Information Technology and the Arts (2000). *Government Online: The Commonwealth Government's Strategy*. Canberra: Department of Communications, Information Technology and the Arts.

Department of Finance and Administration (2006). *Responsive Government: A New Service Agenda*. Canberra: Department of Finance and Administration.

Digital Taskforce (2002). *Towards E-Government: Vision and Strategy for the Public Sector in Denmark*. Copenhagen: Digital Task Force.

Digital Taskforce (2004). *The Danish E-Government Strategy 2004–06*. Copenhagen: Digital Task Force.

Dutton, B. (1999). *Society on the Line: Information Politics in the Digital Age*. Oxford: Oxford University Press.

Edelman, M. (1967). *The Symbolic Use of Politics*. Urbana, IL: University of Illinois Press.

Edelman, M. (1977). *Political Language. Words that Succeed and Policies that Fail*. New York: Academic Press.

European Commission Directorate General for Information Society and Media (2005). *Online Availability of Public Services: How is Europe Progressing?* Brussels: European Commission. Directorate General for Information Society and Media.

Fountain, J. (2001a). *Building the Virtual State*. Washington, DC: Brookings Institution.

Fountain, J. (2001b). The paradoxes of public sector customer service. *Governance*, *14*(1), 55–73.

Gartner Consulting (2000). *Rules and Realities in E-Government*. Retrieved from www.gartner.com May 2003.

Gazendam, H. W. M. (1993). *Variety Controls Variety. On the Use of Organization Theories in Information Management*. Groningen: Wolters-Noordhoff.

Hague, B. N., and Loader, B. (1999). *Digital Democracy: Discourse and Decision Making in the Information Age*. London: Routledge.

Homburg, V. M. F. (1999). *The Political Economy of Information Management: A Theoretical and Empirical Study on the Development and Use of Interorganizational Information Systems*. Groningen: SOM.

Homburg, V. M. F. (2000). Politics and property rights in information exchange. *Knowledge, Policy and Technology*, *13*(3), 13–22.

Homburg, V. M. F., and Bekkers, V. J. J. M. (2002). The back-office of e-government (managing information domains as political economies). Paper presented at the HICSS, Waikoloa Village, Waikoloa, Hawaii.

Jensen, C. B., and Lauritsen, P. (2005). Reading digital Denmark: IT reports as material-semiotic actors. *Science, Technology and Human Values*, *30*(3), 352–373.

Kettl, D. F. (2000). *The Global Public Management Revolution: A Report on the Transformation of Governance*. Washington, DC: Brookings Institution.

Kling, R. (1987). Computerization as an ongoing social and political process. In G. Bjerkness, P. Ehn and M. Kyng (eds) *Computers and Democracy*. Avebury: Aldershot.

Knights, D., and Murray, F. (1992). Politics and pain in managing information technology: A case study in insurance. *Organization Studies*, *13*(2), 211–228.

Kraemer, K. L., Dickhoven, S., Tiernet, S. F., and King, J. L. (1987). *Datawars: The Politics of Modeling in Federal Policy making*. New York: Columbia University Press.

Kraemer, K. L., and King, J. L. (1986). Computing and public organizations. *Public Administration Review*, *46*(special issue), 488–496.

Kumar, K., and van Dissel, H. G. (1996). Sustainable collaboration: Managing conflict and collaboration in interorganizational information systems. *MIS Quarterly*, *20*(3), 279–300.

March, J. G., and Olsen, J. P. (1989). *Rediscovering Institutions*. New York: The Free Press.

Mason, R. O., and Mitroff, I. I. (1981). *Challenging Strategic Planning Assumptions*. New York: Wiley.

Minister for the Cabinet Office (1999). *Modernising Government*. London: Minister for the Cabinet Office.

Minister for the Cabinet Office (2000). *E-Government: A Strategic Framework for Public Services in the Information Age*. London: Minister for the Cabinet Office.

Minister for the Cabinet Office (2005). *Transformational Government: Enabled by Technology*. London: Minister for the Cabinet Office.

Ministeriet for Videnskab Tecknologi og Udvikling (1996). *The Info-Society for All–the Danish Model*. Retrieved from www.fsk.dk/fsk/publ/1996/it96-uk/inde0002.htm January 2006.

Ministeriet for Videnskab Tecknologi og Udvikling (2000). *Digital Denmark–Conversion to the Network Society*. Copenhagen: Ministeriet for Videnskab Tecknologi og Udvikling.

Ministry of Economic Affairs (1999). *The Digital Delta*. The Hague: Ministry of Economic Affairs.

Ministry of Research and Information Technology (1995). *From Vision to Action*: *Info-Society 2000*. Copenhagen: Ministry of Research and Information Technology.

Ministry of the Interior and Kingdom Relationships (1999). *Action Program for Electronic Government*. The Hague: Ministry of the Interior and Kingdom Relationships.

Ministry of the Interior and Kingdom Relationships (2002). *Contract with the Future*. The Hague: Ministry of the Interior and Kingdom Relationships.

Moon, M. J. (2002). The evolution of e-government among municipalities: Rhetoric or reality? *Public Administration Review*, *62*(4), 424–433.

Mosco, V. (2004). *The Digital Sublime*: *Myth, Power and Cyberspace*. Cambridge, MA: MIT Press.

Norris, D. F., and Moon, M. J. (2005). Advancing e-government at the grassroots: Tortoise or hare. *Public Management Review*, *65*(1), 64–75.

OECD (2003). *The E-Government Imperative*. Paris: OECD.

Parsons, W. (1996). *Public Policy*: *An Introduction to the Theory and Practice of Policy Analysis*. Aldershot: Edward Elgar.

Ringeling, A. (2001). Rare klanten hoor, die klanten van de overheid. In A. M. B. Lips and H. van Duivenboden (eds) *Klantgericht werken in de publieke sector. Inrichting van de elektronische overheid*. Utrecht: Lemma.

Schudson, M. (1998). *The Good Citizen*: *A History of American Civic Life*. New York: The Free Press.

Snellen, I. T. M., and van de Donk, W. B. H. J. (1998). *Public Administration in an Information Age*: *A Handbook*. Amsterdam: IOS Press.

Tapscott, D. (1995). *The Digital Economy*: *Promise and Peril in the Age of Networked Intelligence*. New York: McGraw-Hill.

Tat-Kei Ho, A. (2002). Reinventing local governments and the e-government initiative. *Public Administration Review*, *62*(4), 434–444.

Treasury Board (1997). *Strategic Directions for Information Management and Information Technology*: *Enabling 21st Century Service to Canadians*. Retrieved from www.gol-ged.gc.ca May 2003.

van de Donk, W. B. H. J. (1998). Beyond incrementalism. In I. T. M. Snellen and W. B. H. J. van de Donk (eds) *Public Administration in an Information Age*. Oxford: IOS Press.

van Venrooij, A. (2002). *Nieuwe vormen van interorganisationele dienstverlening*. Delft: Eburon.

Zuurmond, A. (1998). From bureaucracy to infocracy. In I. T. M. Snellen and W. B. H. J. van de Donk (eds) *Public Administration in an Information Age*. Amsterdam: IOS Press.

7   ICT evaluation

Key points

After reading this chapter, you will be able to

* explain the importance of evaluation of ICT applications and uses in public administration
* name conventional methods of evaluation, and explain why they often do not suffice when applied to ICTs and to public administration
* name and explain specific difficulties and pitfalls in ICT evaluation methods
* explain what suitable approaches of evaluation of ICT initiatives in public administration can be identified.

Introduction

In previous chapters, ICT, organizational and institutional change have been discussed in the context of information societies, organizations in general, and bureaucracy in particular, in inter-organizational relations and in e-government initiatives (of all flavours). One of the more crude questions one can ask is what we can expect from ICT applications. In Chapter 1, I have argued that this question is indeed crude and more difficult than is apparent at first sight, and at least raises questions about what kind of reasoning one uses in the relation between ICT and public administration (technological determinism, social shaping of technology). Having said this, this does not render the original question less relevant.

If one raises the point of impact, effects, measurement and the like, one raises the question of how to assess – preferably in a systematic way – outcomes of e-government initiatives, technological projects or programmes. These questions are often presented under the heading of 'evaluation'. In general, it can be said that 'performance', 'impact' and 'evaluation' are rather thorny issues (Powell, 1992), both in organization theory and public administration as well as in the discipline of information systems.

In organization theory and public administration, there has been a long tradition of evaluating whether technology improves organizational and policy performance. Despite the interest, both in practice and research, there is no consensus regarding either preferred methods of evaluation or ways to define 'performance'. The meaning of performance in relation to technology apparently is not a truth that is buried somewhere waiting to be discovered if only our concepts and data collection methods were good enough. The perceived complexity of the construct *performance* can probably explain the decrease in popularity of performance in research. Many overviews on organizational performance are referring mostly to literature of the early 1980s, indicating that progress in the area has diminished since then. Some authors even claim that the question of what organizational performance is has slipped off the research agenda since then.[1] Kanter and Brinkerhoff (1981: 321) articulated this belief rather cynically: '[s]ome leading scholars have expressed impatience with the very concept of "organizational performance", urging researchers to turn their attention to more fruitful fields'.

In the discipline of information systems, the issue of 'performance' has been paid attention to, especially due to clamour for accountability because of ICT investments and subsequent expectations. King's (1988) framework of eight evaluation criteria is the basis for much subsequent work on performance (King, 1988; Lederer and Sethi, 1991). Yet in classic information systems handbooks, chapters on how to evaluate information systems, ICTs and technology application, and a discussion on available methods of assessment, are notably lacking.[2]

In this chapter, the difficulties and possibilities of evaluation of ICTs in public administration are analysed and discussed. This chapter is structured as follows. First the concept of evaluation is introduced and various types of evaluation studies are identified. Second, known pitfalls and difficulties of ICT evaluation are discussed, and then the focus is on typical examples of evaluations of ICT in public administration. As always, the chapter ends with conclusions.

Case vignette 7.1: ICT costs

In the Netherlands, annually 5 billion euros are spent on ICT initiatives that are not realized. Experts have estimated that of all national ICT initiatives, 30 per cent is never actually realized, 50 per cent of all projects meets serious problems, and only 20 per cent can be qualified as successful.

An example of a failed ICT initiative is the use of ICT in Dutch police organizations for the purpose of sharing data. Since the early 1990s, 25 regional police organizations have tried to consolidate their information systems in such a way that each regional police organization could access information about suspects from other police organizations' information systems. An ICT budget of 430 million euros did not help. In an investigation, the Netherlands Court of Audit concluded that none of the regional police organizations had an interest in a shared system, because a shared system (in the perception of the police organizations) would downtone the individual organization's policing performance.

A definition and some distinctions

Borrowing from the academic discipline of public administration, evaluation can be defined as the systematic analysis of public policies, programmes and projects (Pollitt, 2003). In a way, especially governments have always evaluated and evaluation in some parts of government is a rather frenetic activity.

In general, it is possible to distinguish between various approaches and various methods of evaluating. First, there is a distinction between ex ante and ex post evaluations.

Ex ante evaluation is defined as the predictive evaluation which is performed in order to estimate and evaluate the impact of future situations (Remenyi, 1999). In this kind of approach of evaluation, it is attempted to estimate (beforehand) what costs, benefits, impacts, opportunities and difficulties will be. Its main purpose is to support system justification. Ex post evaluation, on the other hand, usually assesses the impact of the implemented ICTs, in terms of economic value, social impact, or any other possible outcome.

Second, there is a distinction between formative and summative evaluation. Formative evaluation is typically conducted during the development or implementation of a specific ICT project. Its main purpose is to inform developers and initiators of the characteristics of the project and the progress (or lack of progress) in the development or implementation. Reports of formative evaluation typically are internal documents in which lessons learnt are formalized for immediate use. It can of course be said that many people that are actually involved in development or implementation are constantly involved in informal formative evaluation processes. Summative evaluation is typically done when an application has been implemented, and assesses the impact of ICTs.

Case vignette 7.2: The productivity paradox

Nobel Laureate Robert Solow remarked in 1987 that computers appear everywhere except in productivity statistics. This quotation not only refers to doubt about whether ICTs lead to productivity growth, but also has inspired academics to empirically study productivity growth as caused by applications of ICTs. These kinds of studies have been inspired by the productivity slowdown that began in the early 1970s, at the same time when computers began to appear massively in industry, in the services sector, and in public administration.

Generalized patterns of studies have shown that throughout the 1990s, productivity growth has decreased. More detailed studies have shown that in the United States, white collar sectors, where ICTs have been broadly implemented, have displayed stronger slowdown than in the blue collar sector.

Various explanations have been proposed to explain these observations (Brynjolfsson, 1993):

- *Measurement issues*: although productivity is a simple concept – amount of output produced per unit of input – it is notoriously difficult to measure. For example, the sort of benefits one would expect from ICTs, namely service quality, increased timeliness, responsiveness, are precisely the aspects of output measurement that are poorly accounted for in official productivity statistics. Furthermore, it is very difficult to measure inputs – ICT stock, software, training of employees and so forth.
- *Lags:* another explanation is that benefits resulting from ICTs can be observed only several years after the technologies have been implemented. This makes it difficult to combine outputs and inputs in one measure. Strassman (1985) has repeatedly argued that effects, if any, are noticeable only over periods as long as decades.
- *Redistribution and dissipation of benefits:* the third explanation is that ICTs may be beneficial for individual organizations or citizens, but unproductive for society as a whole. Popularly phrased, ICTs rearrange the shares of the pie without making the pie bigger. For instance, ICTs may be used for monitoring societal problems and gaining insight into the nature of problems, while adding nothing to output measured in financial terms.
- *Mismanagement of technology:* the fourth and final explanation is that potential benefits of ICTs disappear because of mismanagement, duplicated information systems, or in general organizational slack instead of outputs (for an application in public administration, see De Jong, 1994).

One of the leading scholars in the field of productivity studies, Erik Brynjolfsson, has asserted that measurement issues and time lags have been sufficiently dealt with and that it is now clear that productivity gains in the USA since the mid-1980s are due to ICTs.

Third, there is a distinction in ways *how to evaluate* (in other words, what drives the evaluation). With respect to various ways how to evaluate, Cronholm and Goldkuhl (2003) identify goal-based evaluation, goal-free evaluation and criteria-based evaluation.

Goal-based evaluation assumes that there are specific organizational goals that can be identified and that serve as yardsticks for assessing results. The focus thus is on intended results (a percentage of all citizens being content with service provision, a specific level of complaints, a percentage of the population that administers taxes online). In general, such an approach is rather formal-rational in nature and presupposes that measurable goals exist and can be used in evaluation studies. In general, technological determinism is presupposed: technology is assumed to produce results (exogenously), and the results can be observed, measured, and contributed to ICT application. Goal-free evaluation, on the other hand, is a more interpretative approach, in which the focus is on social systems (societies, organizations) with embedded ICTs. The emphasis in this kind of evaluation is to involve a plethora of stakeholders, and to gather as much information of a variety of outcomes as possible. By doing so, evaluators avoid the risk of missing unanticipated yet important outcomes, eliminate tunnel vision and are able to maintain a rather independent position (vis-à-vis the organization that commissions the evaluation) (Patton, 1997). Criteria-based evaluation focuses on assessing the interaction between information systems and users, or citizens in general. In practice one can think of using a checklist to assess a municipal website; such a checklist might include items like: does the website allow for interaction between politicians and citizens, is the navigational structure clear, to what degree is one-stop shopping actually implemented, and so on. There are specific criteria, but they are not derived from organizational or policy goals.

Fourth, there is a distinction in ways *what to evaluate*. Cronholm and Goldkuhl identify evaluation of ICT-as-such, and of ICT-in-use. In the former case, the evaluation is focused on evaluation of the system (the artefact per se) without any involvement of users. Typically, the evaluation is focused on the functionality of the system under investigation. In the latter case, the actual use of the system by users, clients or citizens is the object of study. So the question is not what ICT could produce in terms of outputs, but what outcome actually results when behaviour of stakeholders (citizens, users) is being assessed.

Fifth, there is a distinction in level of aggregation that is the focus of the evaluation. Smithson and Hirscheim (1998) identify the following levels.

1   *Macro / societal level*: this level refers to a national or societal level at which effects are to be noted. In general, this is a very abstract level. In terms of metrics, evaluators often seek to define and operationalize the construct of quality of life, societal cohesion, trust and access (Bannister and Remenyi, 2003).
2   *Sector level*: this level relates to a specific level of administration, for example municipalities in a specific country. An example is the measurement of service quality among various municipal service counters.
3   *Organizational level:* this level refers to the effects typically assessed within a specific organization, for example the timeliness of tax rebates by a national tax authority.
4   *Application level:* here, the focus of the evaluation is a specific ICT application, for example a customer intake module for a local public health authority. Assessment of this level takes place by focusing on the functionality, outcomes or design of the application alone.
5   *Stakeholder level*: at this level, it is explicitly recognized that various stakeholders have various interests and values, which strongly influence their appreciation of specific ICTs. At this level, impacts are measured within groups of specific stakeholders.

Pitfalls of evaluation in practice

Evaluation of ICTs in practice raises many problems, some of which are operational (evaluation is time consuming, it is hard to come up with articulated criteria for evaluation) and some of which are rather fundamental. Below, some of the more fundamental problems of evaluation in public administration are discussed. According to Powell (1992), these kinds of difficulties explain why so many formal evaluations of ICT initiatives in public administration are so unpopular.

Goal diversity

In the public sector as well as in the private sector, organizations have multiple objectives. Municipalities have a number of objectives, varying from enforcement of environmental legislation to delivery of public services, and from providing affordable housing to promoting economic activity. It is in general very hard to indicate what the ultimate goal is to be used in specific evaluation activities.

Cost measurement difficulties

Many ICT evaluations aim to measure costs of ICT initiatives. ICT expenditure, however, is notably hard to measure and in practice, cost calculations vary from evangelical to vaguely apocalyptic. Questions that are raised include:

- Should training costs be included?
- How should depreciation of hardware and software be included?
- Does the cost estimation include development as well as maintenance activities?
- How should the costs of organizational change that occurs as a result of ICT implementation be appreciated?

Benefits measurement difficulties

Even more difficult than measuring costs of ICT initiatives is the assessment of benefits. Thankfully for evaluators, it is possible to assess tangible benefits that result from specific ICT applications, such as staff time savings, reduced communication costs and increased capability to detect errors in operations. On the other hand, there is ample evidence that many ICT initiatives result in intangible benefits (for example in public service delivery). Examples of intangible benefits are

- increased citizens' trust in government
- increased public accountability and legitimacy of policies
- improvement of the reputation of public administration (for example, a specific agency that uses ICT to improve the fairness and motivation of administrative orders, or the use of ICTs to fight fraud in the delivery of social benefits)
- increased citizen participation in policy making, improved access to public information and increased transparency of government
- the fostering of a truly joined-up government and realization of one-stop shops
- improved communication and information sharing within and between governments.

Related to the problem of which benefits to include, is the decision which time frame to use. The impact of ICT initiatives in the short term may be quite different from the impact on the long run. The salient question of course here is what exactly is meant by 'short term' and 'long run'.

ICT investments are investments in infrastructures

Many ICTs initiatives nowadays, be it a municipal website, or a document handling system, are part of an ICT infrastructure instead of that they support a specific, isolated and relatively easy to define organizational function. Systems based on networks, such as electronic service delivery portals, may be highly costly to install and may produce few direct benefits but indirectly they may account for a key part of the organization's information infrastructure and hence account for many future innovations.

Measuring strategic ICTs

In some cases, ICTs are portrayed as necessarily 'strategic' and defined in such a way that it is almost by definition impossible to assess (Powell, 1992). For example, for some public sector organizations, the move to single window, electronic service can be regarded as strategic as it involves a repositioning of that specific organization not only with respect to its base of customers or citizens but also with respect to other public and/or private sector organizations. The impact of such a transition is very hard to assess.

Cynicism and lethargy

Public sector ICT initiatives are prone to failure, partly because of the issues mentioned above, partly because failures are more visible than ICT failures in the private sector. This has, according to Powell (1992), led to a climate of cynicism, in which failure of current ICT initiatives is immediately linked to series of past ICT disasters. Consequently, evaluation becomes a ritualistic activity with very slim chances of actually contributing to organizational and/or institutional learning.

Existing approaches

Introduction

The limitations documented in the previous section might lead to the conclusion that evaluation of ICT applications is impossible. There is, however, a plethora of evaluation models available and these models are in fact employed in public administration around the world. The message here is that each of these available models has to come to terms with the difficulties and pitfalls documented above. In order to illustrate what possibilities of evaluation exist in practice, below, two quite distinct approaches are described. The first one evaluates national e-government policies; the second is an assessment of specific municipal websites.

E-Government benchmark studies

A popular field of study nowadays is the assessment of how various national governments are doing in terms of e-government activities. Several evaluation studies and approaches exist (Janssen et al., 2004). Many of these studies were commissioned out of a concern for comparison and are presented as benchmarks; some have a temporal character because of the recurrent (yearly or bi-yearly) replications of the research. Janssen et al. (2004) analysed a great many country comparisons and concluded that several indicators were used for the purpose of evaluating e-government policies. These indicators include:

- *input indicators*, such as ICT spending as a percentage of total national budget and amount of financial resources devoted to Internet infrastructure;
- *output indicators*, such as number of online public services for citizens, number of online services for private enterprises, percentage of government agencies with websites, and percentage of government agencies that offer transaction services;
- *usage indicators*, such as numbers or percentage of citizens or enterprises that have used online public services, number of online payments, or even percentage of Internet traffic that pertains to electronic public service delivery;
- *impact indicators*, such as citizens' satisfaction with online public service delivery and reduction of waiting time experienced by citizens trying to obtain services from municipalities;
- *environmental indicators*, including ICT penetration in households, schools and private enterprises, indicators for trust of citizens in online transactions and levels of communication costs.

Janssen et al. (2004) concluded that various benchmarks employed various indicators, output and environmental indicators being the most 'popular' sets of indicators. Especially those studies that define e-government as online service delivery seem to employ output indicators. It is these same studies that mostly include a competitive e-government country ranking.

Website assessment

Another typical ICT evaluation activity in public administration that is increasingly prevalent and popular is the assessment and comparison of governmental (in most cases, municipal) websites. A very general model of assessment and evaluation is a methodology aimed at categorizing specific websites in stage models (Garson, 2006). In the Netherlands, the Ministry of the Interior and Kingdom Relations commissions a so-called continuous monitor with which the quality of websites of municipalities, regional governments, water authorities and national ministerial departments is assessed. Assessment takes place by scoring websites based on a number of criteria, that are formalized in a questionnaire. Criteria that are being used can be grouped in a number of clusters. These clusters are:

- user friendliness, measured with indicators like the presence of a search engine, availability and active maintenance of a list of frequently asked questions, presence of a privacy statement, and information about the update frequency of the contents of the website;
- transparency, measured in terms like availability of official announcements, facilities like email alerts when relevant announcements are posted, access to local parliament's information systems, availability of information about local regulations and zoning plans, availability of politicians' weblogs, and facilities for filing complaints;
- availability of information services and transaction services regarding waste disposal, tax services, social benefits, environmental permits, etc.;
- availability of personalized, citizen-centred services like possibilities to track and trace the handling of requests by civic servants;
- accessibility in terms of compliance with national, technological website guidelines and standards, including disability access ('Bobby analyses').

The Dutch assessment is comparable to the approach proposed by McClure, Sprehe and Eschenfelder (Garson, 2006) which focuses on US federal websites. It is important to note here that evaluations of government websites are almost without exception criteria-based evaluations: they measure and assess specific ICTs using sets of criteria that are not related to objectives or organizational goals, and typically do not assess cost-benefit ratios.

Conclusion

In conclusion, I can summarize that ICT evaluation in general, and ICT evaluation in public administration in particular, remains a thorny issue. I have argued that there exists a great variety of approaches in evaluating ICTs, with specific pitfalls and problems that render almost every attempt to assess ICT difficult. Examples of these pitfalls and problems are the goal diversity that is almost endemic to any public agency and that makes it difficult to come up with consistent sets of indicators, difficulties in estimating costs and especially benefits of ICTs in public administration, atypical, immeasurable benefits when ICTs are used in the context of public administration and policy making such as increased transparency and increased levels of citizens' trust in government, and so forth.

Nevertheless, using two brief descriptions of existing evaluation approaches, the assessment of national e-government policies and the evaluation of website quality, I have shown that it is possible to evaluate ICT in public administration using criteria-based evaluation techniques and multiple criteria. These descriptions do not serve to indicate that there are no pitfalls in these approaches; rather, when used with care, and when taking into account known problems and pitfalls, these kinds of evaluation studies can provide useful insights into problems of ICT programmes and projects.

Discussion questions

1   Do you think goal diversity is also relevant for private sector organizations attempting to evaluate ICT initiatives? Why (not)?
2   Explain what kind of evaluation results from (or is compatible with) a technological determinist line of reasoning.
3   Explain what difficulties are imminent when adopting a social shaping of technology perspective, such as is the case throughout the chapters in this book.
4   Name and discuss at least three operational problems of estimating costs and benefits of ICTs, and at least two more fundamental problems of estimating costs and benefits of ICTs.
5   Discuss advantages and disadvantages of criteria-based evaluation methodologies.

Notes

1   A notable exception is the research on competitive advantage itself and the relation between ICTs and gaining competitive advantage in the private sector. However, this topic seems to show a fading interest, too (Breukel, 1996).
2   A notable exception is Chapter 14 of *Public Information Technology and E-Governance* (Garson, 2006), which is a contribution at the cornerstone of information systems and public administration.

References

Bannister, F., and Remenyi, D. (2003). The societal value of ICT: First steps towards an evaluation framework. *Electronic Journal of Information Systems Evaluation, 6*(2), 197–206.
Breukel, A. W. V. (1996). *Strategic IT, but not by ITself*. Groningen: SOM.
Brynjolfsson, E. (1993). The productivity paradox of information technology: Review and assessment. *Communications of the ACM, 36*(12), 67–77.
Cronholm, S., and Goldkuhl, G. (2003). Strategies for information systems evaluation: Six generic types. *Electronic Journal of Information Systems Evaluation, 6*(2), 65–74.
de Jong, W. M. (1994). *The Management of Informatization*. Groningen: Wolters-Noordhoff.
Garson, D. (2006). *Public Information Technology and E-Governance*. Sudbury: Jones and Bartlett.
Janssen, D., Rotthier, S., and Snijkers, K. (2004). If you measure it they will score: An assessment of international eGovernment benchmarking. *Information Polity, 9*(2), 121–130.
Kanter, R. M., and Brinkerhoff, D. (1981). Organizational performance: Recent developments in measurement. *Annual Review of Sociology, 7*, 321–349.
King, W. R. (1988). How effective is your information systems planning? *Long Range Planning, 21*(5), 103–112.
Lederer, A. L., and Sethi, V. (1991). Critical dimensions of strategic information systems planning. *Critical Dimensions of Strategic Information Systems Planning, 22*, 104–119.

Patton, M. Q. (1997). *Utilitisation-focused Evaluation: The New Century Text*. Thousand Oaks, CA: Sage.

Pollitt, C. P. (2003). *The Essential Public Manager*. Maidenhead: Open University Press.

Powell, P. (1992). Information technology evaluation: Is it different? *Journal of the Operational Research Society, 43*(1), 29–42.

Remenyi, D. (1999). *IT Investment: Making a Business Case*. Oxford: Butterworth-Heinemann.

Smithson, S., and Hirschheim, R. (1998). Analysing information systems evaluation: Another look at an old problem. *European Journal of Information Systems, 21*(7), 158–174.

Strassman, P. (1985). *Information Payoff: The Transformation of Work in an Electronic Age*. New York: The Free Press.

8 Conclusions and reflection

Key points

After reading this chapter, you will be able to

- identify how, at various levels of aggregation, technology and institutions and power structures are intrinsically linked to one another
- describe what the relevance of a 'social shaping of technology' (SST) perspective is for discussions about e-government and e-governance
- reflect on implications of an SST perspective for e-government research and practice.

Introduction

This book started with a simple question ('How do ICTs affect public administration?'), a question so simple, the answer simply had to be complicated. Indeed, as I have tried to argue, the question is susceptible to the criticism that it is overly deterministic, ignores relevant reverse causality ('How does public administration affect ways of ICT use?') and ignores how development, form, pace of change and impacts are determined by a variety of factors.

Throughout the chapters, I have demonstrated how technology shapes and is shaped by a variety of factors and contexts, and I have demonstrated the relevance of a 'social shaping of technology' perspective. In this final chapter, I confront and combine insights from various chapters and reflect on the contents and usefulness of the 'social shaping of technology' perspective for the relation between ICTs and public administration. The chapter is structured as follows. First, various conceptualizations of ICTs are discussed and reflected upon. Then, the interactions between the 'social' and the 'technological' at various levels of aggregation (societal, the level of national policy initiatives, organizational and inter-organizational) are identified and commented upon. Some of the main insights and contributions of various chapters for the relation between ICT and public administration are then discussed. The chapter ends with an overview of implications for contemporary issues of ICT in public administration.

Reflection on conceptualizations of ICTs

Throughout the chapters in this book, several conceptualizations of information and communication technologies have been presented.

In Chapter 2, I began by introducing ICTs in the context of a computational view of technology (Orlikowski and Iacono, 2001): the capabilities of symbol representation, symbol manipulation, communication, information processing, and subsequent modelling and simulating aspects of the world were vital to the idea of the Turing machine.

In the same chapter (in the discussion on automating and informating) and in Chapter 1, however, a different connotation is introduced, that of technology as a *tool* that provides specific information processing capabilities. Through information processing capabilities, technology can act as a labour substitution tool and as a productivity tool (see Chapter 7, and Chapter 6 for the use of the tool metaphor in e-government rhetoric).

Most of the chapters, however, have presented a 'social shaping of technology' perspective, which includes, among other things, economic institutions (Chapter 3), national policies (Chapter 6), the development of organizational arrangements (Chapter 4), incentives and power relations (Chapter 5), and so forth. More specifically, to use Orlikowski and Iacono's (2001) terms, technology was conceptualized as an *embedded system*. Technology, in this view, is neither an independent nor dependent variable but instead is seen to be enmeshed with the conditions of its application and use in public administration and public policy.

It has never been the purpose to propose inconsistent conceptualizations of the ICT artefact. Rather, by developing or at least using various conceptualizations it was attempted to theorize about the meanings, capabilities and uses of ICTs in public administration, and to indicate how ICTs increasingly become interdependent with socio-political, economic and institutional contexts and practices. Bekkers and Homburg (2005) extend the embedded 'social shaping of technology' perspective and refer to an information ecology. An information ecology can be described as the evolving interactions and relations between a diversity of actors, their practices, values and technology within a specific and local (thus unique) environment. It is important to stress that in this view, social and technological aspects of an environment co-evolve: public administration and societies at large will continue to be confronted with newer, faster and different tools and services – not once, but repeatedly. Information ecologies evolve as the new ideas and tools arise and people respond to them. They learn and adapt, create and re-create. Hence, there is a continuous process in which elements of the social and technological environment co-evolve (Nardi and O'Day, 1999).

Having identified some basic characteristics of the social shaping of technology perspective, the exact economic, institutional and socio-political factors with which technology is interdependent yet remain to be scrutinized. Therefore, in the subsequent section, these interrelations are scrutinized at various levels: the societal level of the Information Society, the level of national e-government policies, and the level of organizations and inter-organizations.

Social shaping at various levels of aggregation

Social shaping at societal level

In Castells' rendition of the Information Society (see Chapter 3), there seems to be a technological determinist flavour to the line of reasoning: the development of technology is hardly given attention to, and seems to occur independently from the struggle between informational capitalists, the dynamics of legitimate and criminal digital economies, and the clash between hypercapitalism on the one hand and cultural identities on the other hand. Technology drives economic activity and allows for a distinction between In and Out, and yet it simply appears from nowhere.

Nevertheless, Castells does pay attention to ways in which ICTs are actually used, and how its use is dominated by economically advantaged network enterprises, corporations and networked nations for the purpose of consolidating and extending their positions. Its use, therefore, is intrinsically linked with social systems of global producers and networked governments. In this sense, ICTs are not primarily technological artefacts but they are symbolic to the hegemony of the economic and political elite ('the powers that be') in a globalized world.

Technology is therefore, in Castells' view, intrinsically embedded in the values and practices of economic and political elites who use ICTs to expand their power and to enable hypercapitalism.

Social shaping in e-government policies

In Chapter 6, e-government was defined as the redesign of information relationships between government agencies and their environments, in many cases citizens. In the various national e-government programmes (at a *rhetoric level*), and at the shopfloor of many agencies throughout the world, it can be noted that of all possible types of redesign, there is a preference for using a managerial model, which fosters client orientation and focuses on service delivery rather than on participatory services and consultation of the general public. Here we witness how specific values (in this case, the values of *customer orientation*, *responsiveness* and *focus on public services and products*) shape the actual implementations of e-government initiatives.

Social shaping at organizational and inter-organizational levels

In Chapter 2 in the discussion of organizational intelligence, two alternative scenarios were identified: a first one in which technology was put to the creative hands of empowered workers who were freed from direct, tangible interventions by senior management, and a second one in which technology was used by senior management to heighten and enforce control over processes and workers. Technology here embodies both the potential of empowerment as well as the potential of *control*, depending on whoever masters the technology.

In Chapter 4, it was shown how technology rendered much of the operational logic (a quest for control for the purpose of efficiency) of the ideal type of bureaucracy irrelevant. Because of technology, job specialization, narrowly defined tasks, and even organizational boundaries could be contested. Another value, however, that of maintaining clear lines of authority for the purpose of enabling accountability, still proved to be relevant.

Chapter 5 featured how information exchange and blurring of traditional boundaries resulted in practice in 'data wars' and 'battle of back offices'. Unlimited access to information resources was fiercely fought by various organizations. In terms of neo-institutional economics: organizations attempted to regain residual property rights of information assets as much as possible to avoid being controlled by other organizations. In terms of organizational-political logic, organizations tried to minimize their dependence on other organizations, at the same time trying to make other organizations as dependent as possible on themselves. Here, again, it can be observed how technology plays a role in attempts by specific actors to achieve control over others.

The web of technology, power and institutions

This book's central contribution is its development and application of a 'social shaping of technology' perspective to the relation between ICT and public administration. The concepts of technology, institutions (that is, values and commonly accepted practices) and power (the ability to achieve control over others) developed and described in the various chapters, neatly fit in with the 'social shaping of technology' perspective as described by Williams and Edge (1996). These authors focus on choices (although not necessarily deliberate choices) inherent in the design of technologies, as well as in the direction or trajectory of application. Hence, different routes are available, and the character and form of technology as well as its implications are opened up for inquiry (Williams and Edge, 1996).

The issues of control and power (see previous section) are explicitly addressed by the 'critical strand' and 'political economy strand' within the broad church of 'social shaping of technology' in which authors like Bruno Latour and Lawrence Winner (see also case vignette 1.2) argue that technologies are fostered by specific actors to preserve or alter social and political relations. In general, cross-organizational, cross-sectoral and cross-national comparisons are promoted in order to explain both particular forms and uses of technology, as well as various implications. In Chapter 6, such a cross-national scrutiny of e-government policies was presented.

Existing literatures have, until now, paid attention to technology, power and institutions, however these sources mainly focus on public utilities, very specific technologies like parallel computing technology, and the commodification of software, to name a few examples. A notable exception here is a study by Heeks and Stanforth (2007) in which the authors attempt to explain the trajectory of an Integrated Financial Management Information System in the Sri Lankan public administration. Heeks and Stanforth (2007) explain how power relations in global and local networks of actors can be used to explain the specific trajectory the development of the system has taken. Examples of studies like this one are desperately needed to inform how ICTs shape and are shaped by the power relations, institutions and social and economic factors endemic to public administration.

Outlook

From the insights of the various chapters in the book, and from the academic disciplines of public administration, organization theory and information systems that informed the main line of reasoning set out in this book, a number of specific implications for the development and use of ICTs in public administration can be identified, as well as a number of implications for the ways in which public administration changes because of ICTs. They are reported below.

The first one is that *any* application of ICT is developed, implemented and used in interaction with actors with specific roles, values, incentives and interests. Hence, the definition of the problem for which a technological solution is sought, as well as the form of the technology that is being implemented and used, is the result of interactions in which different meanings are exchanged, discussed or enforced. Power, institutions and social and economic factors play an important role in the selection and adaptation of ICTs in public administration.

The second one is that if we accept that technology is intrinsically embedded in a web of power relations, institutions, values and economic and social factors, the meaning, shaping and effects of ICTs are situated in a local (as opposed to a general, global) context. Therefore, benchmarks of e-government (see p. 118) should be interpreted with great caution. More often than not, it is attempted to derive requirements for e-government championship from these benchmarks, and this is of limited value as requirements are highly interwoven with specific institutions and power relations. Obviously, Montreal's e-government lessons do not necessarily apply to Rotterdam, and there may be sound reasons for Germany not to copy the UK e-government's policies.

The third one is that in many ICTs, there is an embodiment of the potential to control. In the 'social shaping of technology', there is ample discussion regarding the question whether this potential is 'autonomous' and control is technologically determined or whether it is constructed in use. The position taken here is that control in ICTs can be activated and utilized by specific actors to control other actors or specific purposes.

The fourth one is that if one uses a 'social shaping of technology' perspective, any form or trajectory of technology can be expected and any future form or trajectory is unpredictable. Until now, specific relations between characteristics of technology on the one hand and institutional, social, economic and political factors on the other hand have not been identified and still have to be explored. One way of doing this is to scrutinize and compare technologies in various settings, be it countries, sectors or organizations. These kinds of comparative studies could help to progress our knowledge of how *exactly* social shaping of technology takes place. Furthermore such studies could also inform us of what exact constellations of actors, interests, power bases and control potentials stimulate, mediate or obstruct technology in public administration, or administrative reform.

From these insights, an understanding of the complex relation between ICT and public administration has been presented. I hope that an appreciation of the roles of the academic disciplines of information systems, organization theory and public administration in understanding this relation will urge students of these disciplines to progress and to inform one another of accomplishments. Furthermore, it is hoped that future system developers, organization scholars, public executives and public managers will be better equipped to deal with the challenges of 'e-government'.

References

Bekkers, V. J. J. M., and Homburg, V. M. F. (2005). The information ecology of e-government: Background and concepts. In V. J. J. M. Bekkers and V. M. F. Homburg (eds) *The Information Ecology of E-Government: E-Government as Institutional and Technological Innovation in the Public Sector*. Amsterdam: IOS Press.

Heeks, R., and Stanforth, C. (2007). Understanding e-government project trajectories from an actor-network perspective. *European Journal of Information Systems, 16*, 165–177.

Nardi, B. A., and O'Day, V. L. (1999). *Information Ecologies: Using Technology with Heart*. Cambridge, MA: MIT Press.

Orlikowski, W. J., and Iacono, C. S. (2001). Research commentary: Desperately seeking the 'IT' in IT research: A call to theorizing the IT artifact. *Information Systems Research, 12*(2), 121–134.

Williams, R., and Edge, D. (1996). The social shaping of technology. *Research Policy, 25*, 865–899.

Index